THE SONG O

A contemplative guide

—◆◆◆—

Graeme Watson

Sara

With love and prayers.

Graeme.

19ᵉ July 2014

First published in Great Britain in 2014

Society for Promoting Christian Knowledge
36 Causton Street
London SW1P 4ST
www.spckpublishing.co.uk

The author and publisher have made every effort to ensure that the external website
and email addresses included in this book are correct and up to date at the time
of going to press. The author and publisher are not responsible for the content,
quality or continuing accessibility of the sites.

Unless otherwise noted, Scripture quotations, including the Song of Songs, are
taken from the New Revised Standard Version of the Bible, Anglicized Edition,
copyright © 1989, 1995 by the Division of Christian Education of the National
Council of the Churches of Christ in the USA. Used by permission. All rights reserved.

Every effort has been made to seek permission to use copyright material reproduced
in this book. The publisher apologizes for those cases where permission might not have
been sought and, if notified, will formally seek permission at the earliest opportunity.

British Library Cataloguing-in-Publication Data
A catalogue record for this book is available from the British Library

ISBN 978–0–281–06690–2
eBook ISBN 978–0–281–06691–9

Typeset by Graphicraft Limited, Hong Kong
First printed in Great Britain by Ashford Colour Press
Subsequently digitally printed in Great Britain

eBook by Graphicraft Limited, Hong Kong

Produced on paper from sustainable forests

To my parents,
Hubert (1906–74) and Audrey Watson (1910–89),
also to Carol (1939–92) and Liz (born 1951),
deux belles femmes, adorables et formidables

Contents

Acknowledgements

I wish to acknowledge the following authors, poets and publishers for their permission to quote from the following:

Church House Publishing for permission to quote the collect for All Saints Day in *Common Worship*. Extracts from *Common Worship* are copyright © The Archbishops' Council, 2000, and are reproduced by permission. <copyright@c-of-e.org.uk>

Continuum Publishing (now part of Bloomsbury Publishing) and Dr Peter Tyler for permission to quote from his translation of *The Spiritual Canticle* in *St John of the Cross*.

Joy Cowley for her personal permission to quote her contemporary version of Mary's song (Magnificat), reprinted from *Mirabile Dictu* (21 December 2007).

Darton, Longman and Todd for W. H. Vanstone's poem 'Love's endeavour, love's expense' from *Love's Endeavour, Love's Expense* (1977).

Enitharmon Press for U. A. Fanthorpe's poem, 'Friends Meeting House, Frenchay, Bristol'.

Oxford University Press for Sister Edmée Kingsmill's translation of biblical texts in *The Song of Songs and the Eros of God* (2009); also 'Lord of all hopefulness' by Jan Struther (1901–53) from *Enlarged Songs of Praise* 1931; also 'There is a flower springing', words freely translated by Ursula Vaughan Williams from *The Oxford Book of Carols* © Oxford University Press 1928. Extracts reproduced by permission of Oxford University Press. All rights reserved.

Perpetua Press for Rowan Williams' translation from the Welsh of two poems, 'Hymn for the Mercy Seat' and 'I saw him standing', by Ann Griffiths (in *The Poems of Rowan Williams*), and for his own personal permission.

St Paul's Press for the translation of the poem 'O God you pour yourself in your gift!' by Mechthild of Magdeburg.

Westminster John Knox Press, for Ellen Davis's translation of biblical texts in *Proverbs, Ecclesiastes, and the Song of Songs* (2000), and for her own personal permission.

Acknowledgements

Following these formal acknowledgements, there are many other people I wish to thank for their help and interest in this project. First, Alison Barr, my commissioning editor, for her encouragement and patience, and indeed all her colleagues at SPCK for their meticulous care, suggestions for improvement and alluring cover design. Second, Sister Edmée Kingsmill SLG for her personal interest and challenging face-to-face 'tutorials'. Her profound scholarship and prayerful wisdom have been foundational and intrinsic to my writing of this book. Third, Professor Ellen Davis of Duke Divinity School, whose nuanced commentary on the Song of Songs has been informative and inspirational.

I have greatly benefited from a number of workshops, quiet days and retreats with several groups of practising meditators associated with the Christian Meditation community in the UK. Many thanks to all of these for their insights and enthusiasm. Again, I wish to thank the diverse group of people who have read parts of my book in its early stages, and made extensive and valuable comments. They are James Ashdown, Sally Barnes, Gina Garrett, Jonathan Gebbie and Isabelle Glover. My thanks also go to those who have shown special interest and support. They include Julienne McLean, my spiritual director, Dom Laurence Freeman, Director of the World Community for Christian Meditation, and the members of St Mary's Stoke Newington Christian Meditation Group.

Throughout the course of this project I have been aware of the loving and prayerful support of my nearest and dearest, especially my sister Diana and her husband Ron of Christchurch New Zealand, and my brother David and his wife Diane in England. Above all, I owe more than I can possibly express to my beloved wife Liz for her own insights, critical comments, and whole-hearted and unstinting spiritual companionship and practical support at all times. This book is dedicated to her, and also to my late equally beloved wife Carol, who as an accomplished Hebrew scholar would certainly have been closely involved had she been able to. As it happens, 2014 would have been the fortieth anniversary of our wedding, as it is also the twentieth of my present marriage. These close relationships are of course deeply connected to the theme of this book, which draws on my own experience of 'love as strong as death'. It is again 40 years since my father's death, and 25 years since my mother's, the two people from whom I first experienced the unconditional love that is ultimately a reflection of divine love. It is to their memory also that this book is dedicated.

About the author

The Revd Graeme Watson is an Anglican priest who has worked in pastoral posts in this country and overseas, and in training men and women for ordained and lay ministries. A spiritual director, he leads poetry workshops, quiet days and retreats, and is the author of *Strike the Cloud: Understanding and Practising the Teaching of the Cloud of Unknowing* (SPCK, 2011).

Introduction

The Song of Songs is one of the smallest books in the Hebrew Scriptures. It can easily be overlooked, tucked away after the world-weary
Ecclesiastes, and immediately before the greatest of all the prophets,
Isaiah.[1] For centuries it has been to all intents and purposes hidden
away, hardly ever read aloud in public worship.[2] It is only in the last
few years that it has come out of the cold, and begun to be read
publicly, not least at weddings.

It has not always been so. In the earliest centuries of the Church's
history, this was one of the very best-known and best-loved biblical
books for teachers, bishops, abbots, abbesses, and lay brothers and
sisters in religious communities. Many of the greatest Christian
leaders preached on the Song of Songs, quoted from it, and knew it
intimately. In the eighth century the Venerable Bede of Jarrow wrote
a commentary on it. In the twelfth century St Bernard of Clairvaux
wrote no fewer than 86 sermons inspired by it, covering every subject
from the life of the monks under his care to the papacy and its
problems. The great Spanish mystics of the sixteenth century, St Teresa
of Avila and St John of the Cross, were deeply influenced by the Song,
using it to describe and develop their experience of the spiritual
journey.

Despite being only rarely heard in churches, the Song of Songs has
nevertheless provided inspiration to singers, composers and artists,
both classical and popular. Among classical composers, J. S. Bach's
Advent anthem and hymn 'Sleepers, Wake' uses words and imagery
from the Song of Songs. Vaughan Williams wrote a choral cantata,
Flos Campi (*Flower of the Field*), based on a number of texts from
the Song. Benjamin Britten composed a canticle based on the Song:
'My beloved is mine and I am his'.[3]

In the world of recent popular music, the title of the 2004 album
Catch for Us the Foxes by mewithoutYou, a Philadelphia-based experi-
mental rock band, is taken from chapter 2, verse 15 of the Song.
The group Black Madonnas quotes from the Song (1.5): 'I am black,
but beautiful, O daughters of Jerusalem . . .', while the Israeli pop

superstar Ofra Haza recorded 'שיר הבהא' (Love Song) on her 1988 album *Shaday*. This is a direct quotation of the Song's most famous verses, 8.6–7: 'Set me as a seal upon thine heart, as a seal upon thine arm: for love is strong as death . . .'[4]

The composers of all this music have found in the Song a powerful expression not only of the passion of human love, but also, in some cases, of something else that could be described as transcending erotic love – a deep yearning for unity with the Other, however they might choose to describe that Other: Christ, God, the Universe, Planet Earth.

The Yorkshire Sculpture Park near Wakefield recently had on loan an installation entitled 'Jerusalem' by the Spanish sculptor Jaume Plensa. This sculpture consisted of 11 large bronze gongs, on each of which is inscribed a different verse from the Song. Visitors to the exhibition were invited to sound these gongs. Each gong emitted a different note according to the text carved into it. The deep booming sounds of the gongs are such that they resonate not only in the ear, but reverberate through the whole human body. Given the right conditions, we 'hear' not only in our eardrums but in some deeper place within the body and soul. We hear with the 'ears of the heart', to use St Benedict's phrase.[5]

It is evident that the Song of Songs has a wide appeal beyond those familiar with the Bible. One way in which interest in it both inside and outside faith communities may be revived is through a healthy recognition that a greater familiarity with the poem can help us to bring our sexual and spiritual lives together. From the Garden of Eden story onwards, many biblical texts testify how love can go wrong, but a broader reading of the Scriptures reveals that God's love for his world, and for us human beings, has a passionate aspect, in which erotic language is far from inappropriate. In fact, it is the most apt language of all by which to describe all the different aspects of love.

This is where the Song of Songs is of special significance to all who are interested in the prayer of silence and stillness, the prayer of the heart, centring prayer or Christian meditation. To all those who are being drawn to practise such prayer the Song is a unique biblical resource. The current interest in contemplative prayer, both within and outside the Church, is surely a God-given sign of the times that cannot be ignored. This book has been written in the hope that it may bring to others, as it has brought to me, the gifts of joy, light and peace, and a more profound sense of God's love in our own lives.

The book is divided into two parts, each with a particular purpose.

Part 1

The first part is intended as a further extended introduction to the Song of Songs. The Song was written over 2,000 years ago in a part of the world very different from our own and in a language and within a culture unlike anything we know. It calls for elucidation.

In Chapter 1 there is a discussion about the interpretation of the Song. How is it to be read? Literally or metaphorically? Next there is a chapter on the language of love in poetry, with particular reference to three love songs within the Song of Songs. Chapter 2 also includes a section on the language of the mystic, and the relationship between the language of love and that of the mystic. Because relatively few contemporary, especially non-Jewish, readers will be familiar with the references and allusions that the author and his original audience would have been acquainted with, in Chapter 3 we explore the relationship between the Song and other books in the Bible, especially those within the Wisdom tradition. Lastly, we dip into the writings of some of the most influential commentators on the Song from the second to the sixteenth centuries in order to appreciate something of the weight and power of a metaphorical reading of the poem.

While it is not essential to read Part 1 before embarking on Part 2, its contents may help to overcome some of the barriers that may hinder listening to, or reading, the poem with our minds alert and our hearts alive.

Part 2

> The Song of Songs, attributed to the wise but promiscuous Solomon, is a fragmentary, dream-like poem in which language itself seems smitten by love's excess. It has exerted a profound influence on love poetry throughout the ages.[6]

Carol Ann Duffy's acute observation brings us to the heart of the book's character. Because of its 'fragmentary, dream-like' quality, a straightforward verse-by-verse commentary is not always the most helpful method of study. An alternative approach is to focus on the texts that would appear to strike contemporary readers as particularly illuminating, memorable or enigmatic, not least when the 'language itself seems smitten by love's excess'.

The text of the Song has been divided, somewhat arbitrarily but I hope usefully, into 50 sections. The Song lends itself readily to the practice of *Lectio divina* (divine reading), in which the aim of reading is to allow the text to speak to the heart. In the Appendix, you will find a brief description of this practice. In all circumstances, whether you are alone or with others, you are strongly advised to read the words aloud. Only by hearing them spoken out loud will you appreciate the full flavour and delight of this beautiful gem of a poem.

The sections of text and commentary are in most cases followed by a reflection, a poem or a hymn, or a combination of these.

The poems, hymns and readings selected are intended to illustrate, sometimes to develop, the themes found in the Song. They are mostly taken from English and Welsh poets and writers, from the sixteenth century to the present day. Many of the poets are likely to have been profoundly influenced, consciously or unconsciously, by the Song.

Part 1

1

'My beloved is mine and I am his': a poem of many meanings

Of all the books in Holy Scripture, the Song of Songs is the most mysterious. It appears as a poem, or perhaps a series of poems, in which two unnamed lovers express their admiration of each other's physical beauty in a completely uninhibited and thoroughly sensual way. Various other people are referred to – the woman's brothers, the city police, King Solomon and a group of women of Jerusalem. But they are not central to the poem. The essential motifs are the ups and downs of a new vibrant relationship; the theme of burning passionate love; the pain of separation; the anxiety of searching for, and finding, or not finding, the lost beloved; the joy of rediscovery; the hope, if not yet the full reality, of a final consummation.

There is no evident moral message, nor editorial comment. And although there have been many attempts to find a storyline in the poem none has been convincing. We might be surprised that God is never mentioned, although this omission does not make this book unique in the Hebrew Scriptures. The book of Esther also has no reference to God. But there is a difference. Whereas Esther is closely linked to an annual feast in the Jewish calendar,[1] the Song of Songs has no obvious connection with any such feast or episode in the history of Israel. Nor does the poem, at least on the face of it, have any affinity with the great themes of the rest of the Hebrew Scriptures, such as covenant, slavery, liberation, law, exile and restoration. Although the geographical references are to the land of Israel and its neighbours, it is essentially timeless, and universal in its appeal.

Origin and date

Most biblical scholars are of the view that the poem must date from a period long after the life of King Solomon (1000–931 BCE).[2] It is

3

most likely to have been written and circulated towards the end of the period when the Hebrew Scriptures were being written, between the third and the first centuries BCE, at least some 600 or 700 years after Solomon's death. The name of Solomon was most likely added by an editorial hand after the book had been accepted into the canon of Holy Scripture in order to inform the reader that it is Wisdom literature – Solomon's name being associated with Wisdom.[3] The Christian Church incorporated the Wisdom books, along with the Law and the Prophets, and at a later stage their own Scriptures (the New Testament), into the canon of Holy Scripture.[4]

Meaning and interpretation

The most important question facing the reader of this poem is the question of its meaning. Let me first state what seems to me to be almost, but not quite, self-evident. On the face of it, it appears to be a poem about human love, and this is indeed how most modern commentators have treated it. Thus Stephen Mitchell writes:

> The Song of Songs is a poem about the sexual awakening of a young woman and her lover. In a series of subtly articulated scenes, the two meet in an idealized landscape of fertility and abundance – a kind of Eden – where they discover the pleasures of love.[5]

He suggests that it can be read as a counter to the original Eden story in Genesis, where the loss of innocence is fraught with dire consequences. The Song looks at 'the same border-crossing from innocence to experience . . . and sees only the joy of discovery'.[6] In a similar vein, Cheryl Exum writes:

> The Song of Songs is a long lyric poem about erotic love and sexual desire – a poem in which the body is both object of desire and source of delight, and lovers engage in a continual game of seeking and finding in anticipation, enjoyment, and assurance of sensual gratification . . . The poem's genius lies in the way it shows us, as well as tells us, that 'love is strong as death' and in the way it explores the nature of love. It looks at what it is like to be in love from both a woman's and a man's point of view and it relies exclusively on dialogue, so that we learn about love through what the lovers say about it.[7]

However, the interpretation of the Song as a poem simply and exclusively about human erotic love is relatively modern. In its most widespread form this view is hardly much more than 100 years old. For almost 1,900 years, with one or two exceptions, such an interpretation was neither accepted nor acceptable. A quite different attitude prevailed, one that saw the poem as an extended metaphor of God's love for his people, and their reciprocal love of God. However, by the middle of the twentieth century, the modern interpretation had become the most common way of understanding the Song.

This 'literal' or 'horizontal' interpretation has much to be said for it. The Song celebrates the joy of a loving relationship, with no expectations or presuppositions about marriage or the family. It recognizes realistically that there is no love without pain, but it also affirms that love cannot be bought or bargained for, but must await the right moment for its birth. At the same time, love is as powerful as death. The death of a partner inevitably brings about the grief of separation, but love itself is not extinguished by death; it lives on in the heart and memories of the surviving partner or spouse.

Multiple meanings

Yet however meaningful for many this apparently straightforward reading may be, is there not something missing? A number of contemporary scholars from diverse backgrounds are now putting forward the view that the older interpretation is not so easily discarded, and that the poem may indeed have more than one meaning – perhaps multiple meanings. This book has been written in the conviction that the Song does have other less obvious meanings, and these can transcend even the finest and deepest of human love relationships.

For our present purpose, it is sufficient to recognize that in recent years there has been a rediscovery of the ancient insight that texts can have more than one meaning. The third-century biblical scholar Origen[8] believed that the whole of Scripture was the Word of God, inspired by the Holy Spirit. But he made an important distinction. He recognized that most of the Bible is written in a perfectly plain, morally and spiritually worthy literal sense. It is available to the ordinary Christian. But, he argued, there are some texts that are so odd and anomalous as to demand a spiritual meaning, requiring the neglect of the literal sense, for in such places a literal sense is either missing altogether, being nonsense, or is offensive, or factually incorrect. Origen suggested that these anomalous texts are, as it were, cracks in the surface of the literal meaning, through which may be glimpsed something of the depths of spiritual meaning that underlie and sustain the whole text of the Scriptures.[9] For Origen, the Song of Songs was an anomalous text, because at a literal level it did not make sense to him, but at a spiritual level it made perfect sense. In Part 2 we will return to this point.

Confusing though it may be for those who assume that a Bible text has only one meaning – that is, the 'plain meaning' – there is another important contemporary insight. It is equally important to recognize that all reading takes place within a particular social context and is done by particular people with a particular history and a particular perspective. This is just as true of our reading of the Bible, as of reading any classical texts. In fact, there is no such thing as an objective Bible reading, without a particular perspective, and that includes all our presuppositions and, of course, our individual prejudices. 'Where are you coming from?' is always a legitimate question when anyone presumes to tell us 'what the Bible teaches'. This is why today we find a diversity of interpretations, arising out of different, and sometimes conflicting, perspectives on how God speaks to us through biblical texts.

Moreover, there is always room for growth in our understanding. 'If we keep working on a text, we shall find that our own understanding of it and our reactions to it will change and develop as we continue to grow and find ourselves in new circumstances.'[10] This is another significant insight, which invites further reflection.

Let us take just one example of this diversity of interpretations, that of women's perspective.

Women's perspective

What is especially attractive to women readers when they read the Song is that the central female character sees herself as equal to the man. So, for example, 'the woman takes the initiative in making love and expressing her feelings at least as often as the man,' writes Adrian Thatcher.[11] In fact, it is the voice of the woman, together with the female chorus, which is the most dominant. This is highly unusual in the Hebrew Scriptures, as indeed in the Bible as a whole. So far as we know, the Bible was written by men, and women have no distinctive voice. Another recent commentator, Trevor Dennis, wrote in 1994: 'Over the last twenty or thirty years, however, there has been a flowering of a movement within biblical studies, in which increasing numbers of women have come to see that they have distinctive questions to ask of a text and distinctive insights to offer.'[12]

Could the Song have possibly been written by a woman? Whether that is likely to have been the case or not, the Song will come to many new readers as a welcome breeze of fresh air.

This diversity in interpretation does not mean that all perspectives are necessarily as good, as true, or as creative as each other. Nor does it mean that they are completely subjective, dependent entirely upon the feelings and imaginations of readers. But it does mean that the reader's own experiences of faith and life are likely to play an important part in determining how a particular text is read and understood.

Human love and divine love

The Song, it seems to me, was written within a faith community in which it was natural to celebrate the gift of human love. At the same time it was a community whose members were able to picture the ardent and faithful love of two human beings for each other as pointing to the ardent and faithful love of God for his people, and of the people's love affair with God. But a reading at two levels, or possibly more, depended upon a poet who knew the sacred Scripture. Equally, such a reading depended upon readers who saw the connection between human erotic love and God's passionate love, and who could find support for that connection in the Scriptures and in their own experience of God.

'God is love and those who abide (remain/live) in love abide (remain/ live) in God' is one of the most profound insights in the whole of Scripture.[13] The Song, I believe, is as much about divine love as it is about human love. This insight is not new, and is embedded in the sacred Scriptures of the Jewish people. Furthermore, as we shall see, it was Jewish rabbis who first expressly made the close connection, and their teaching informed and influenced our Christian forebears. The New Testament makes explicit what was already implicit in the Old.

The deepest meaning that can be given to the Song is that it is a lyrical poem about a two-way love-affair – God's overwhelming love for humanity, and the loving response of humanity to that overwhelming love. Our human loving response is, of course, patchy and fragmentary in the extreme, and a cause of sorrow and penitence. Yet in aspiration and hope we can always stand confident: 'The glory of God is a human being fully alive; and to be alive consists in beholding God.'[14]

> In this is love, not that we loved God but that he loved us and sent his Son to be the atoning sacrifice for our sins . . . No one has ever seen God; if we love one another, God lives in us, and his love is perfected in us.[15]

> > My song is love unknown,
> > My Saviour's love for me,
> > Love to the loveless shown,
> > That they might lovely be . . .
> >   Samuel Crossman (1624–83)[16]

Let me remind you again that our wholehearted openness to love is the condition to which you and I and every human being is called. It is the meaning and purpose of our lives. It demands a great deal, but in the end we will find that all we have lost are our limitations.[17]

2

'O God, you burn with desire': the language of the mystic

The language of love is the language of exuberance, movement, change and life. Lovers delight in comparing their beloved with the most admired and beautiful features of the natural and humanly constructed worlds.

> O, my Luve's like a red, red rose
> That's newly sprung in June.
> O my Luve's like the melodie
> That's sweetly played in tune.[1]

Or

> Shall I compare thee to a summer's day?
> Thou art more lovely and more temperate.[2]

The language of the Song seems to be 'smitten by love's excess', and that is why the Song has been admired and quoted by many great teachers in the Christian mystical tradition. Just as lovers cannot find language that adequately expresses the object of their delight, and the preciousness of their relationship, so also mystics are compelled to acknowledge that all language fails when it comes to speaking of the relationship between themselves and God. It is typical that the mystics express themselves in bold, exciting and paradoxical images. And this excess of language leads in only one possible direction – to the holy ground where the only appropriate response is silence and contemplation. On this holy ground, all images, concepts and human formulations must vanish.[3] This is why the Song of Songs offers such a valuable resource for the prayer of silence and stillness, for contemplative prayer.

Let us see how these ideas work out in relationship to the Song. As the poem develops, we hear each of the two lovers waxing lyrically about the beauty of their beloved.

Here is how the male lover first describes his beloved:

> How beautiful you are, my love;
>> how very beautiful!
>
> Your eyes are doves
>> behind your veil.
>
> Your hair is like a flock of goats,
>> moving down the slopes of Gilead.
>
> Your teeth are like a flock of shorn ewes
>> that have come up from the washing;
>
> all of which bear twins,
>> and not one among them is bereaved.
>
> Your lips are like a crimson thread,
>> and your mouth is lovely.
>
> Your cheeks are like halves of a pomegranate
>> behind your veil.
>
> Your neck is like the tower of David,
>> built in courses;
>
> On it hang a thousand bucklers,
>> all of them shields of warriors.
>
> Your two breasts are like two fawns
>> twins of a gazelle,
>> that feed among the lilies.
>
> Until the day breathes
>> and the shadows flee,
>
> I will hasten to the mountain of myrrh,
>> and the hill of frankincense.
>
> You are altogether beautiful, my love;
>> there is no flaw in you.
>
> Come with me from Lebanon, my bride;
>> come with me from Lebanon.
>
> Depart from the peak of Amana,
>> from the peak of Senir and Hermon,
>
> from the dens of lions,
>> from the mountains of leopards.[4]

Listen now to the female lover speaking about her beloved:

> My beloved is all radiant and ruddy,
>> distinguished among ten thousand.

His head is the finest gold;
   his locks are wavy,
   black as a raven.
His eyes are like doves
   beside springs of water;
bathed in milk,
   fitly set.
His cheeks are like beds of spices,
   yielding fragrance.
His lips are lilies,
   distilling liquid myrrh.
His arms are rounded gold
   set with jewels.
His body is ivory work,
   encrusted with sapphires.
His legs are alabaster columns,
   set upon bases of gold.
His appearance is like Lebanon,
   choice as the cedars.
His speech is most sweet,
   and he is altogether desirable.
This is my beloved and this is my friend,
   O daughters of Jerusalem.[5]

And here is the male lover addressing his beloved again:

Return, return, O Shulammite!
   Return, return, that we may look upon you ...

How graceful are your feet in sandals,
   O queenly maiden!
Your rounded thighs are like jewels,
   the work of a master hand.
Your navel is a rounded bowl,
   that never lacks mixed wine.
Your belly is a heap of wheat,
   encircled with lilies.
Your two breasts are like two fawns,
   twins of a gazelle.
Your neck is like an ivory tower.

Your eyes are pools in Heshbon,
    by the gate of Bath-rabbim.
Your nose is like a tower of Lebanon
    overlooking Damascus.
Your head crowns you like Carmel,
    and your flowing locks are like purple;
    a king is held captive in the tresses.

How fair and pleasant you are,
    O loved one, delectable maiden!
You are stately as a palm tree,
    and your breasts are like its clusters.
I say I will climb the palm tree,
    and lay hold of its branches.
Oh may your breasts be like clusters of the vine,
    and the scent of your breath like apples.
And your kisses like the best wine
    that goes down smoothly,
    gliding over lips and teeth.[6]

Modern commentators remark that these particular poems within the Song have the form of a traditional Arabic *wasf* – that is, a highly sophisticated description by the bridegroom of his bride, and vice versa. The origins of *wasf* appear to go back 1,000 years before the Song was composed, to ancient Egypt, and continue to this day in modern Arabic poetry. To Western ears, the description and comparisons may well sound bizarre, even far-fetched. Certainly, the lovers' language is absolutely ecstatic.

One of the features of these love poems is that, although there is plenty of detail, the language and images used do not give the hearer or reader much idea of what the lovers actually look like. This is also true of love poems in other cultures, including our own. In these descriptions what we find is rather the language of powerful feeling. The language used does not describe so much as express the delight of the lover in the beloved. The images of gold, ivory, jewels, sapphires, marble, aromatic spices, dripping myrrh, lilies, doves and cedars, together with features of the landscape such as streams of waters and terraces, are employed to create the effect within a paradisal environment of two god-like people, statuesque, beloved and admired, beyond almost all human comparison. They are used not simply to arouse a sensual response, but to invite the reader to engage lovingly with the world the poet imagines.[7]

There is another point to consider. Even allowing for the vast cultural divide between the world of ancient Israel and our own contemporary Western world, it is quite difficult to see how images like these could in any way be adapted into the language of lovers today. Could these particular lines be recited at a contemporary wedding ceremony? Their exotic character and overwhelming excess of meaning would surely more likely bring about a response of perplexity, even amusement, rather than one of resonant empathy and pleasure. How do we make sense of them in a contemporary context?

Here again, if we look in more detail at these descriptions, we notice that in the first extract the images employed by the poet are unusual in that they are clearly not intended to suggest more than one point of similarity, or at the most, two. If we take as an example, 'cheeks like halves of pomegranates', cheeks only resemble pomegranates because of their healthy reddish colour; and in 'teeth like a flock of shorn ewes', this is true only because teeth are white and relatively uniform in appearance. Again, hair is only like a flock of goats because it is black and moving (surging), or like waving palm trees because of its thick waves and curls.[8] There are just as many, if not more, dissimilarities as there are similarities.

Another unexpected feature that makes the descriptions of these lovers so different from other love poems is the many topographical references. Although the atmosphere is that of an idyllic paradise, with frequent references to a garden, which may be taking us back to the Garden of Eden, or perhaps forward in promise to a future paradise, the actual names are specific to particular places. For the original Jewish readers, these had special associations. Gilead, for example, would have evoked associations with the early foundational period of Israel's history. Here the tribes of Reuben, Gad and Manasseh settled at the end of their 40 years of wandering in the desert. Here too God brought deliverance to Israel through the leadership of Saul, their first king. Later, it became a disputed territory between the kings of Israel and Damascus. The reference to Gilead could therefore function as an assertion of Israel's single undivided identity and power.[9] If these are the associations being invoked, the beloved female is being admired not only for her beauty but also for her strength: a strength given and blessed by God.[10]

Again, the description of the woman's breasts being like fawns feeding among the lilies can hardly be read as an exact simile. In Near Eastern art, the image of fawns with stylized lilies is a standard one, as fawns were sacred to Astarte, the goddess of love. But even a reader who was unaware of this connection would recognize in this simile an image of beauty, evoking admiration.

So we have here a cluster of images associated with both strength and beauty, an exceptionally beautiful and fruitful land, bursting with life, the two lovers sharing it with sheep and goats, gazelles, foxes, lions and leopards.

Some of the places referred to can hardly be understood literally. For example, 'the mountain of myrrh'[11] cannot have been situated within or around Israel, as myrrh does not grow in that region. What the language conveys is rather an imaginary landscape evoked by the description of the woman's body with which myrrh and frankincense are particularly associated.[12] The significance for a mystical interpretation is that these strongly scented spices are also used in the ritual of the Temple in Jerusalem. The strong aromas of myrrh and frankincense call to remembrance the people of Israel's intimacy with God. So, as we read these poems, we may begin to work out that the beloved female does indeed symbolize the Temple itself, while her lover is God.

The beloved Temple

It is impossible to overstate the significance of Jerusalem and the Temple in the religion of Israel, both then and now. We have only to recall that even today the Western Wall is the sole surviving relic of the Temple, and remains *the* holy place for all Jews. We return to this point in the next chapter, and it will be a recurring factor in the commentary in the second part of this book.

That the lover is God and the beloved is the Temple, or Jerusalem, or Israel itself, is confirmed by other considerations. For example, in the second poem,[13] the beloved woman does not venture to make physical contact with her lover. After extolling his outstanding beauty and desirability, she declares simply: 'This is my beloved and this is my friend.' Ellen Davis suggests:

She is practising the kind of reserve characteristic of the best of Israel's theology, which is both modest and daring. Israel modestly refrains from laying possessive claim to God's exquisite beauty, yet dares to imagine that we humans might be a source of pleasure for God.[14]

In each of these love poems, it is natural to be struck by the diversity, abundance and quite extravagant character of the similes and metaphors. In the second poem these range from lilies, grapevines, apples and date palms to wild animals, fawns, gazelles, and then to man-made works of art and skill: a bowl, purple cloth, bands, a gate, an ivory tower. But this again is only one aspect of this extraordinary description. There is the unusual way in which the beloved female is portrayed, in exactly the opposite way from what would be the usual fashion. The poet's eyes move not downwards from her hair, face and eyes, but upwards from her feet to her thighs, her belly, her breasts, neck and facial features.

This carefully crafted description is designed, like the others, to reach beyond even the excesses of a lover's unabashed and daring language to one that goes beyond all human comparisons in order to touch on the divine. To make this point clear, it becomes almost impossible to make sense of them *simply and only* as the language of human love. The language is, however, most appropriate for the divine–human encounter.[15]

In the third poem, the most striking new word we meet is 'Shulammite', on the lips of the male lover, referring to his beloved.[16] The term has puzzled commentators, for it occurs nowhere else in the Scriptures, or again here in the Song. The most likely explanation is that the word was coined by the poet, based on the original name of Jerusalem, which was Salem, or Shalem.[17] If this is so, the poet is thus cryptically confirming the identification of the beloved woman with Jerusalem, where the Temple is to be found. This suggests that the poet is one whose spiritual life embraced the Psalms, where Jerusalem is so central. To the psalmist, Jerusalem is 'the joy of the whole earth'.[18] 'Pray for the peace of Jerusalem: may they prosper who love you.' And Jerusalem's good is to be sought 'for the sake of the house of the LORD our God'.[19]

It is impossible to make sense of the Song unless we extend our imaginations to encompass the central significance to Israel of Jerusalem and its Temple. It is fruitful therefore to reflect on some of the so-called 'Songs of Sion' in the Psalms. Here is one example:

Great is the LORD and greatly to be praised
    in the city of our God.
His holy mountain, beautiful in elevation,
    is the joy of all the earth,
Mount Zion, in the far north,
    the city of the great King . . .

We ponder your steadfast love, O God,
    in the midst of your temple.
Your name, O God, like your praise,
    reaches to the ends of the earth.
Your right hand is filled with victory.
    Let Mount Zion be glad,
let the towns of Judah rejoice
    because of your judgements.

Walk about Zion, go all around it,
    count its towers.
consider well its ramparts;
    go through its citadels,
that you may tell the next generation
    that this is God,
our God for ever and ever.
    He will be our guide for ever.[20]

Before reading the Song we need also to rid our minds of the limitation of seeing the Christian Church simply as a historical institution, deeply flawed and fallible. As the New Testament testifies, in its essential being the Church is called to be the Mystical Body of Christ and the People of God, created and sustained by God to fulfil God's purpose of reconciling the world to himself.

But God who is rich in mercy, out of the great love with which he loved us even when were we dead through our trespasses, made us alive together with Christ – by grace you have been saved – and raised us up with him and seated us with him in the heavenly places in Christ Jesus.[21]

So too the Church is called to be the bride of Christ, and to be nothing less than God's own Temple, the meeting place of God and all humanity. 'Do you not know that you are God's temple and that God's Spirit dwells within you?'[22]

Lord Jesus, here is your body:
It is fallible yet inspiring;
It is flawed yet beautiful;
It is tired yet creative,
And through you it is constantly made new.[23]

These three powerful love poems of the Song, full of ecstatic language and imagery, invite us to a place that transcends all earthly loves: Paradise restored, the mystical vision of God, the mutual delight that may be experienced in an intimate communion of the divine and the human, where truth and beauty have their ultimate union.

3

'O loving wisdom of our God':
a book of holy wisdom

'Wisdom has on the whole not had an easy time in recent centuries in the West,' writes the Cambridge theologian David Ford.[1] But the mental climate is changing. There is a new interest in wisdom, especially where 'knowledge and know-how come up against questions of ethics, values, beauty, the shaping and flourishing of the whole person, the common good and long-term perspectives'.[2]

Wisdom must now be recognized as an essential part of what religion should be about, and what it is to be human in a world of dangerously competing ideologies. And among all the books of scriptural Wisdom, the Song of Songs has a special, perhaps even a unique place.[3]

The Jewish Wisdom tradition and Solomon's Temple

It is now increasingly well understood that the Song cannot be properly appreciated unless read within the broader Jewish Wisdom tradition. Many of its key words, ideas and images are also found within that wider Wisdom tradition.

The Song of Songs was once described by Rabbi Akiva, a Jewish teacher in the second century, as 'the holy of holies'.[4] What he said was: 'the whole world is not worthy of the day that the Song of Songs was given to Israel. For all the Scriptures are holy, but the Song of Songs is the holy of holies.' This assertion, that the Song of Songs is 'the holy of holies', on a par with the most sacred place in the Temple, is an astonishing one, yet it must be taken seriously, for his was not a lone voice. He claimed to be following the teaching of other orthodox rabbis.

In addition to it being given the name of Solomon, indicating that the Song of Songs is a 'Wisdom book',[5] the most important other reason why the Song is called 'Solomon's' may be its associations with Solomon's biggest project – the design and building of the first Temple. In Chapter 2 we discussed how the language of mystical love in the Song may be pointing to the Temple as a symbol of God's love for Israel and of Israel's love for God. Ellen Davis explains that 'although the Temple in Jerusalem is never mentioned directly [in the Song] . . . the cumulative effect of the language and images . . . orients us towards that place of ultimate intimacy with God . . . Further, perhaps the title suggests that the Song is one way of entering that holy place.'[6] This theme is one that will regularly recur in our commentary in Part 2.

We now look in a little detail at some correspondences between the Song and some texts in Proverbs, Sirach and the Wisdom of Solomon, which are significant because they support the connections between the Song, Wisdom and the Temple.

Proverbs and the Song

We begin with a couple of key verses from Proverbs.

> Let your fountain be blessed,
>> and rejoice in the wife of your youth,
>> a lovely deer, a graceful doe.
> May her breasts satisfy you at all times;
>> may you be intoxicated always by her love.[7]

A number of lines in the Song appear to be related, as follows:

> A garden locked is my sister, my bride,
>> a garden locked, a fountain sealed.

> I adjure you, O daughters of Jerusalem,
>> by the gazelles or the wild does,
> do not stir up or awaken love
>> until it is ready!

> Your two breasts are like twin fawns,
>> twins of a gazelle.

> Your love is better than wine.[8]

The resemblances between the Proverbs verses and the lines in the Song have often been noted by commentators. The question is, how do we interpret them? What is the connection between the Song, Wisdom and the Temple?

The first point to note is that in the Bible, breasts are never understood, as they might be by a modern reader, as having erotic significance, but rather as that which provides nourishment, in this case spiritual food. Second, while the word 'intoxicated' might suggest 'getting out of control', here it is qualified by 'always', a word that comes from a root meaning order, regularity or ritual. So the phrase suggests 'sober drunkenness', 'being drunk in the Spirit': a controlled ecstasy, a phenomenon familiar to Christians associated today with the Charismatic movement or with Pentecostal churches. 'The wife of your youth' is the woman who is no stranger or casual acquaintance, but one to whom you committed yourself when you reached adulthood. The text from Proverbs is implying that the true source of human well-being is a committed long-term relationship with Lady Wisdom. This too is a regular theme of the Song.

Several texts from the Wisdom of Solomon express nuptial imagery even more clearly. 'I loved her [that is, Wisdom] and sought her from my youth, and I desired to take her for my bride.'[9] And in Sirach[10] we find this: 'She [Wisdom] will come to meet him like a mother, and like a young bride [literally, the wife of his youth] she will welcome him.' This lawful and desirable wife, then, is Lady Wisdom.

The reference to 'a lovely deer, a graceful doe' is also significant.[11] In the Song the daughters of Jerusalem are solemnly charged: 'I adjure you . . . by the gazelles or the wild does: do not stir up or awaken love until it is ready!'[12] In the Hebrew Scriptures, to take an oath involves calling on the God of Israel to act as guarantor. Here in the Song, these wild, elusive and swift creatures would seem to represent God because they represent Wisdom, and Wisdom is an aspect of God.[13]

In another significant and related text from Proverbs,[14] a young man lacking in good sense, ignoring Lady Wisdom, is deceived by Lady Folly into committing adultery, and comes to a sticky end. The scene is one of *night*, in a *street*, and in *broad ways*. A strange woman meets a man. She *seizes* him, *kisses* him, and claims she has made peace *offerings*. 'I have decked my *bed* . . . and sprinkled it with *myrrh, aloes and cinnamon* . . . let us drink our fill of *love* until morning; let us delight ourselves with *love*.' The words in italics here are all to be found in the Song.[15] The Song is also the only other book in the Bible in which these three spices – myrrh, aloes and cinnamon – are grouped together.

While presenting a stark contrast to the Song in its description of an illicit sexual encounter, a comparison shows that the whole passage has clear resemblances in its vocabulary and situation to verses in the Song.[16] It may, of course, be read as a straightforward cautionary tale, but when we recall that the theme of adultery is one commonly used by the prophets as a metaphor for idolatry, these verses may also be interpreted as a warning about the dangers of disordered emotion and passion: misdirected *eros*, leading to the worship of false gods. Such *eros* is to be contrasted with the love for Lady Wisdom, which leads to worship of the true God and brings salvation. It may be that the Song was in part deliberately written as a counter-text to the bleak words in Proverbs, and to the frequent warnings about idol worship in the Prophets. We return to this point later.

Sirach and the Song

Some particularly interesting parallels exist between the Song of Songs and the book of Sirach. Gerhard von Rad observes: 'the description of a lover who pursues the beloved and encamps near her house . . . and glances through her window, listening at her door, resting in her shade . . .' is to be read as a metaphor for the wise man's pursuit of truth personified as the Lady Wisdom.[17]

This dynamic pursuit of wisdom may be compared with an image found in the second chapter of the Song.

> Look, there he stands
>   behind our wall,
> gazing in at the windows,
>   looking through the lattice.[18]

Other passages in Sirach also seem to have a close literary connection with the Song.

> She will come to meet him like a mother,
>   and like a young bride she will welcome him . . .
> He will find gladness and a crown of rejoicing.[19]

Compare in the Song:

> Look, O daughters of Zion,
>   at King Solomon,
>   at the crown with which his mother crowned him
>   on the day of his wedding,
>   on the day of the gladness of his heart.[20]

There are some even more significant connections with Sirach. For example, Gerald Sheppard notes that 'in the Song of Songs . . . a young woman appears in a garden rich with the same kinds of vegetation as that in Sirach 24'. He goes on:

> The garden is filled with costly perfumes and spices; in its centre a fountain is fed by the plentiful streams of Lebanon. Either at the close, or periodically within the different garden scenarios of the Song of Songs, the lover offers a summons to partake of the produce of her garden. Sirach 24 has these same motifs of flora, spices, garden rivers and a call to indulge in the lavish fruits of the garden.[21]

Sheppard remarks that 'the more important question concerns how this imagery of Eden-like splendour relates to the overriding theme of Wisdom's journey, like Israel, to Zion'. We will return later to this theme of the relationships between Wisdom, Jerusalem and Eden, which are central for an interpretation of the Song as a metaphorical poem about God's passionate love for his people.

Wine, milk, honey

All three elements – wine, milk and honey – are frequent images in the Song. They are also encountered in many of the Wisdom writings and usually serve a metaphorical purpose. The common factor with wine, milk and honey is that they have each undergone a transformation from materials in a raw or simple state to products in a more refined or complex condition.[22] A hidden process happens in each case. Thus they readily become symbols of the hidden transformation that has to happen at the level of the spirit if the raw material of the human person is to develop that capacity for discernment about which Isaiah writes: 'He shall eat curds and honey by the time he knows how to refuse the evil and choose the good.'[23]

It is hardly necessary to add that from a Christian point of view this is precisely our understanding of the transforming nature of both the sacraments and the Word of God, which are outward signs of God's love.

Wine occurs in the Song seven times. In the first chapter, wine is implicitly on a par with milk.[24] Wine and milk are unambiguously good gifts, but there is a better one: 'your breasts are better than wine'; and again, 'we will remember your breasts more than wine'. As stated earlier, breasts always connote a source of nourishment. In the second chapter the woman relates that the man has brought her to 'the house of wine', a phrase unique to the Song; as we shall see in Part 2, this may be interpreted as the Temple or, implicitly, a state of prayer.[25] In the fourth chapter the man applies to the woman the very same terms as she applied to him in the first chapter:

> How fair are your breasts, my sister, my bride;
> how much better your breasts than wine.[26]

Again, in the fifth chapter, honey, wine and milk are referred to together in the same sentence, when the man says:

> I eat my honeycomb with my honey,
> I drink my wine with my milk.[27]

It is a commonplace in both Jewish and Christian traditions that milk, and therefore breasts, and honey are all to be understood as metaphors for spiritual sustenance. It is in that light that we may also read the lines:

> Your lips distil nectar, my bride;
> honey and milk are under your tongue.[28]

The Song and the rest of the Hebrew Scriptures

It is impossible here to do justice to the many textual links between the Song and the rest of the Old Testament and its Apocrypha. Suffice to say that there are more than 150 such cross-references and allusions to the texts of the Psalms and to the book of Proverbs, and over 200 to the prophetic books.[29]

The case, then, for the Song of Songs being 'directly and consistently biblical',[30] an integral part of the Wisdom writings, and a counter-testimony to the warnings of the Prophets, is powerful. Ellen Davis sums it up like this:

> the Song is a mosaic of quotations from other parts of scripture. Phrases from the Prophets, the Torah [the Law], and the Psalms abound . . . not just scattered words, but in many cases connected phrases – vivid images and terms too specific for their other contexts to be forgotten by those familiar with biblical language.[31]

For our purposes, it is particularly important to note that the Song of Songs relates especially well to those elements of the Wisdom literature that are open to being interpreted as poems celebrating God's Wisdom personified as a female presence. Lady Wisdom is intimate with God, but also available to human beings as a guide, a mother, a bride (and sometimes, crossing the gender divide, even as a bridegroom), one to be embraced with passion and joy, being both the lover and the beloved. So the Song transcends the categories of human love, rising to the heights of 'Love Divine, all loves excelling.' At the same time, divine love can only be communicated to human beings once they know, through their own personal experience, what love is: its transports of delight, its pitfalls, its ecstasy, anguish, disappointments, heaven, purgatory, finitude and eternity. The Song opens up this whole range of human experience.

The Christian Wisdom tradition

The significance of all this for the practice of contemplative prayer cannot be overestimated, for the whole aim of this prayer of the heart is to reach unity with the divine. In that aim, as the New Testament testifies, there is no need to seek God in any particular place, whether temple, cathedral or your local church building. 'The hour is coming, and is now here, when the true worshippers will worship the Father in spirit and truth, for the Father seeks such as these to worship him.'[32] Our Temple and our Jerusalem are not located on any map, but in the hearts of those who seek God in spirit and truth. So the image and idea of 'the Temple' as a place of intimacy with God is still hugely relevant.

It comes as no surprise, therefore, that the title *The Temple* was given to the collection of 175 poems in which the priest-poet George

Herbert (1593–1633) explored the ups and downs of a personal relationship with God.[33] For Herbert, and other Christians of his time, the Song of Songs was an allegory[34] of the relationship between Christ and his Church, and within that bond, the relationship of the individual believer with God. This is the rationale and model for his poems, in which the poet, like the psalmist, sees himself as a representative of the community of faith.[35]

The essence of Christian wisdom may be summed up like this. The pursuit of wisdom must, above all, be in learning to love God for God's sake, grounded in 'a theology which seeks a wisdom of worship, prayer and discerning desire that is committed to God and the Kingdom of God'.[36]

Metaphor and allegory

Up to now we have used the term 'metaphorical reading' to refer to the interpretation of the Song as being, at one level, about divine love. We need now briefly to explore the term 'allegory', referred to just now. Allegory and metaphor are not the same. A metaphor, which may be expressed in a single word, is used to present an idea in an arresting, convincing or intelligible way. Allegory, literally 'other wording', is 'usually a narrative in which the true meaning is to be got by translating its persons and events into others that they are understood to symbolize. *The Faerie Queen* and *The Pilgrim's Progress* are allegories.'[37] An allegory, therefore, is a complex extended metaphor. It often has a purpose of teaching, whether explicit or implicit. The author of the Song of Songs may or may not have deliberately intended to write an allegorical poem – it is impossible to be sure. What is certain, as we have seen, is that for the best part of 19 centuries Jewish rabbis and the overwhelming majority of the teachers of the Christian Church read the Song of Songs as an allegory of the love of God for God's people, and the reciprocal love of God's people for God. This reading includes God's personal love for the individual, and vice versa.

One common misunderstanding concerning the Song is the assumption that the only way in which such an erotic poem could have been admissible within Holy Scripture is that it had to be read exclusively as an allegory. This is not the case. Allegory was used as an alternative way of reading Scripture and other ancient texts, but never as the only way. Referring to the Song of Songs, the Old Testament scholar

John Barton says that 'allegorical reading in ancient times was prac-
tised precisely on books that [already] had a high status'.[38] At least
two parables in the Gospels are to be read as allegories, while St Paul
explicitly uses allegory more than once, clearly assuming that his
readers would understand this as a normal method of reading sacred
Scripture.[39]

The important point is this: the Song of Songs was given an allegorical interpretation not in order to make it admissible within sacred
Scripture, but because an allegorical reading elevated the theme of
passionate human love to a higher level of meaning.

There are, however, some problems with reading any text allegorically. If the author does not expressly indicate to readers, or make
it obvious, that this is how the words are to be interpreted, we cannot
be sure that they were intended to be read that way. We do not know,
of course, what the author of the Song intended, or what his original
readers would have understood, and that is why a many-layered interpretation is to be preferred. Second, readers are always at liberty to read
into a text what they like or prefer. While this approach could easily
degrade into a licence for eccentricity, fruitless speculation and con-
fusion, in the case of the Song this is not such a problem as it might
otherwise be. Although unique in its style and content, we know that
the Song does not stand alone. It has to be read within the context
of all the Jewish Scriptures. This in turn informs the way in which
it should be interpreted within the Christian dispensation. In the
Christian scheme of things, Christ is the central figure, and is therefore
both the Lover and the Beloved, while the Church, herself represent-
ing the whole of humanity, is also both the beloved and the lover.

4

'God unknown, he alone calls my heart': the mystical tradition

————◆•◆•◆————

Throughout the first 19 centuries of the Christian era, as we have seen, it was the allegorical and mystical interpretation of the Song that dominated both Jewish and Christian thinking. We now briefly explore a representative number of such teachers. But before we look at the Christian tradition, a few comments about the Jewish mystical tradition are necessary, for it was Jewish rabbis who pioneered this way of reading the Song.

The Jewish mystical tradition

At the heart of the Jewish faith is the obligation to love God, which must have within it a powerful element of desire, a desire to please God and to be united to God. 'At its best this obligation is not a burden, but is simply living out Israel's true character and identity, for Israel lives by and for and from God's freedom and passion,' writes Walter Brueggemann.[1] Likewise, there is a strong passionate, emotional element in the words used to describe God's love for Israel: 'God has set his heart on you.'[2] So God's commitment to Israel is a personal one that has 'a dimension of affection and in which God is emotionally extended for the sake of Israel'.[3] It is true that the translations of the Hebrew word for love (*hesed*) – 'steadfast love', 'compassion' and 'mercy' – found throughout the Hebrew Scriptures do not have the same emotional component as our phrase 'passionate love'. Nevertheless their frequency is an indicator of their central significance in Hebrew teaching. God's steadfast love, compassion and mercy are a vital and integral part of the biblical message from Genesis to the Psalms, from Isaiah and Jeremiah to Hosea.[4]

It is from such a scriptural basis for the centrality of steadfast love, compassion and mercy that the mystical tradition within Judaism can be traced. For example, if we take the significance of the beloved's yearning for a kiss in the opening verse of the poem, one Jewish scholar comments that 'the kiss is the culmination of a spiritual quest, a rapture of the perfected soul into divine bliss. Several puns underscore the point . . . the phrase "let him kiss me" is heard to hint at the soul's purification and cleaving to God.'[5]

Another important theme in the Jewish mystical tradition is that of the spiritual marriage. The term spiritual marriage, used to describe the highest degree of contemplative prayer experienced by the mystic, has a long history. Benedicta Ward writes: 'The use of the image of marriage to describe the union of the soul with God is to be found also in pre-Christian sources, both Jewish and Platonic.' The Jewish biblical scholar Philo of Alexandria (c.20 BCE–c.50 CE) saw the union of the soul with God in nuptial terms. Again Benedicta Ward comments: 'It is, however, in the Old Testament that the image of a spiritual marriage is most clearly used in describing the relationship of God to Israel.'[6] This tradition can be most clearly seen in Isaiah and Hosea.[7]

The Christian mystical tradition

Building on these Jewish sources, Christian theologians and mystics developed this idea of the spiritual marriage between God and humanity. The Song of Songs was, and still is, read as describing two separate but related themes: the spiritual marriage between Christ and his Church, and at a more personal level the mystical experience of the individual soul, culminating in the personal spiritual marriage with God. We can trace these two themes in a number of influential teachers, beginning with Origen in the third century, and continuing with Ambrose of Milan, Gregory of Nyssa and Augustine of Hippo in the fourth and fifth centuries, Gregory the Great in the sixth century, the Venerable Bede in the eighth, St Bernard of Clairvaux in the twelfth, and St Teresa of Avila and St John of the Cross in the sixteenth.

The enormous influence these teachers had on the mainstream Christian tradition will soon become clear.

Origen (c.184–253)

The earliest of these, Origen of Alexandria,[8] was notable as a brilliant scholar of the Bible. During his lifetime he had an international reputation, travelling widely, even teaching at the imperial court in Rome. After his death, his daring and speculative thinking was thought by mainstream theologians to be problematic, and as a result his reputation suffered and much of his work was lost or destroyed. But enough has been preserved to reveal something of the immense contribution he made to biblical scholarship. Andrew Louth summarizes:

> Here was a wealth of reflection on Scripture that could not be ignored, and, as the ground of his mystical theology, was to be deeply pervasive in its influence. For him the Song of Songs was *the* book on the summit of the mystical life. Among the many topics he discusses are the union of the soul with God, and the idea of the three stages of the mystical life, later called purificatory, illuminative, and unitive – and the notion of the spiritual senses.[9]

For Origen the biblical books of Wisdom form a threefold pattern of teaching. Thus Proverbs teaches 'moral science, the proper manner of virtuous living'; Ecclesiastes presents what he called 'natural science, that is enlightened knowledge of the nature of things and of how they are to be used as God intended'; while the Song of Songs is that which describes mystical theology. It is the textbook for inner discipline, the interior life of the spirit. In Origen's own words, it is the book that 'instils love and desire of celestial and divine things under the image of the Bride and the Bridegroom, teaching how we come to fellowship with God through paths of love and charity'.[10]

Origen was aware of the danger of reading the Song at a literal or 'carnal' level, and therefore he advised that it should be read only by the spiritually mature. Developing St Paul's distinction between life lived according to the flesh – that is, apart from God – and life in the Spirit,[11] Origen taught that there is a distinction between the outer person, subject to corruption, and the inner person, destined for eternal life, and an obligation for the mature Christian to rise from the letter to the spirit, saying that 'besides our bodily senses, there exist in human beings five other senses'. The contemporary Greek Orthodox teacher Kallistos Ware comments:

> [Origen] talks about a sensuality that has nothing of the senses in it; a higher sense faculty, a divine sense perception. The soul has its eyes, ears, and its sense of taste, of smell, of touch. And

these spiritual senses need to be developed in the inner life. Through this language [Origen] is trying to express the richness and variety of the Christian life. We don't just hear the word of God, we can also 'see' God. We can 'taste' him. We can 'smell' him. We can 'touch' him. There is a great variety of inner experience. Christ our God is not just apprehended in abstract conceptual terms through the reasoning brain but also through feelings, through inner sensations. He is known in a personal, experiential way.[12]

Here in Origen we also find a distinction made between physical love, in which the lover sows in the flesh, and spiritual love, by which the inner person sows in the spirit. He teaches that 'the soul is moved by heavenly love and longing when, having clearly beheld the beauty and the fairness of the Word of God, it falls deeply in love with His loveliness and receives from the Word Himself a certain dart and wound of love'.[13] We return later to this theme of the dart and wound of love.[14] For now it is sufficient to note the significance of the Song for him, and the desirability of reading it allegorically as the finest account of the interior life of the Christian.

St Ambrose of Milan (c.337–97)

Ambrose began his working life as a civil servant, rising to the post of governor of Milan and the province of which it was the hub. On the death of the bishop of Milan, the laity of the diocese demanded that he should be appointed as his successor. Ambrose was most famous as a preacher. While he could hardly be described as a mystic in the modern sense, he was the author of many Latin hymns and as such had a great ability to compose memorable poetry that has been long-lasting.

In his interpretation of the Song, Ambrose built on Origen's work. Although he wrote no commentary, he refers to the poem so often that practically every verse of the Song is mentioned somewhere among his writings. Here are just two examples of his teaching, both from his book about the Hebrew patriarch Isaac.

Ambrose refers to the early verses of the Song, making a connection between the bride's entry into the king's chambers and St Paul's account of his rapture to paradise.

Blessed is the soul that enters the inner chambers. For rising up from the body she becomes distant from all, and she searches and seeks within herself, if in any way she can pursue the divine. And when she can obtain it, having passed beyond intelligible things, she is strengthened in it and fed by it. Such was Paul, who knew that he had been caught up into paradise but did not know whether he had been caught up in the body or out of the body . . . and he was alienated from himself and held within himself the ineffable words which he had heard and could not reveal, because, as he remarked, it was not permitted to speak such things.[15]

In a later chapter Ambrose outlines four stages of spiritual progression, which he takes from the Song.[16] The kiss (Song 1.2), followed by the entry into the king's chamber (1.4), symbolizes the first initial experience by the bride of the divine.[17] This is followed by the sudden departure of the bridegroom, 'in the midst of conversation', who soon returns but in a new way. 'For as she was seeking, he came leaping over the mountains and bounding over the hills.' Ambrose writes: 'And she went forth at his word, and finally (through wounds, the wounds of love) she found and held on to the one she sought so as not to lose him.'

Here Ambrose is outlining the landmarks of a common experience of the spiritual journey: the experience of Christ's presence followed by an absence that increases the soul's desire, and the soul's resolution to purify herself through the practice of goodness. Ambrose found this pattern to be inherent in the text of the Song. It is a pattern that was later developed in the work of two great twelfth-century mystical writers, St Bernard of Clairvaux and William of St Thierry, who explored the dialectic of God's presence and absence, which they too had found in the Song.[18]

St Gregory of Nyssa (*c.*335–*c.*395)

A contemporary of St Ambrose, St Gregory of Nyssa (in modern Anatolia) wrote a commentary on the Song of Songs. Gregory was a thinker, a biblical scholar, and theologian of great originality, learning and spiritual depth. 'His mystical theology is now recognized as one of the most powerful in Christianity.'[19]

His commentary on the Song consists of 15 homilies. He sees the Song as a 'guide for every type of philosophy and knowledge of God'.[20] The Song is interpreted as expressing the soul's constant yearning for the divine Logos (God's Word incarnate in Christ) and the human possibility of getting nearer to Christ. The theme of the goal of the Christian life being the endless pursuit of God in God's inexhaustible nature is for him amply illustrated in the Song. In the twelfth of his homilies, he writes:

> When she hoped, like Moses, that the king's face would appear to her (Exod. 33.13–22), the one whom she desired escapes her grasp. She says, 'my beloved has passed by' (Song 5.6), but he did so not to forsake her soul's desire, but to draw her to himself . . . The bride never ceases going in nor going out, but she rests only by advancing towards that which lies before her and by always going out from what she has comprehended.[21]

Thus Gregory, like Ambrose, brings out the paradoxical character of every perception of the divine presence as an experience of a presence that is also an absence.

The Venerable Bede (673–735)

From when he was a young child Bede lived, worked and wrote within the monasteries of Wearmouth and Jarrow in County Durham. He felt that he was living at the furthest frontiers of the globe, far from the world of the Church fathers of previous centuries, but remarkably he had access to most of the Christian tradition through its literature, commentaries and Scriptures. He was determined to make known these treasures to his own people, the newly converted Angles and Saxons. But Bede was not as interested as the early fathers were in the higher reaches of personal prayer. He was more concerned with practical charitable action, saying: 'Very few ascend to the contemplative, and these the more sublime ones [do so] after [achieving] perfection in good deeds.'[22]

His approach to his commentary on the Song of Songs was to take the matter of salvation and see how the text of the Song applied to the contemporary reader. The words of the Song were always for him a gateway to understanding something important about the character and nature of Christ, or about what it means to be a disciple of Christ, or indeed both. This does not mean that Bede ignored the literal and grammatical meaning of the Song; he goes into some detail about the nature of the various spices mentioned, for example. And he was especially careful to explain that the erotic language of the Song was not to be misunderstood. He does not begin with the act of physical love-making and use the text to explore that. 'He begins with the concept of divine love that is God in Christ redeeming the world to himself, and the transfiguration of human desire towards him.'[23] The meaning is to be found not *in* the outward sense of the image, but *through* the image to its true inner meaning. Take the text, 'His cheeks are like beds of spices'. He sees 'cheeks' as the index of character shown in the face, and here as a reference to Christ, whose cheeks register his emotions, whether exaltation, grief, tears or compassion. He views 'beds of spices' as an orderly display offering charm and fragrance to all who need or want it: in other words, they too symbolize Christ, God made man, whose teaching is sweet to the hearers.[24] However, Benedicta Ward comments:

> It was not so much that each word would lead the reader to see the beauty of Christ and his message, but that the Spirit of God would illuminate the true meaning of every word, and in the process of absorbing the words, the reader would become more ready to be changed by him.[25]

St Bernard of Clairvaux (1090–1153)

St Bernard of Clairvaux was the most celebrated churchman of his day, wielding immense influence not only on the development of his own Cistercian Order of monks, but on the papacy itself at a critical time of dispute and dissension. But it is in the 86 sermons on the Song of Songs, written and revised over many years, that his main claim to fame resides. In these his subject matter ranges from the practical life of the monk to the mystical relationship between the bride and the bridegroom he found in the Song. The bridegroom is Christ, while the bride is variously interpreted as the Church or as the human soul. His interpretation was hugely influential not only on the life of contemporary religious orders; it survived even the Reformation until the seventeenth century and beyond.

Here are three examples of Bernard's teaching. On the text 'In my bed night after night I sought him whom my soul loves', he comments, 'the Bridegroom has not returned when the Bride calls him back with cries and prayers. Why not?' The first answer he gives is this: 'He wishes to increase her desire, test her affection, and exercise her faculty of love. He is not displeased with her, he is concealing his love. But he has been sought for, and we must ask whether he may be found, for he did not come when he was called.'[26]

Bernard develops these reflections further. He underlines the beloved's eager longing.

> How great must be her longing and her ardour, that she does not blush to rise in the night and be seen running through the city, questioning everyone openly about her beloved, not to be deflected for any reason from her search for him, undaunted by any obstacle, undeterred by any desire for rest . . . Yet in all this she is disappointed of her hope. Why? What is the reason for this long unrelenting disappointment, which induces weariness, foments suspicion, inflames impatience, and acts as a stepmother to love and a mother to despair? If he is still concealing his love, it is too painful.

This is fine writing. Bernard is a master of the spiritual life, and here he explores the depths of anguish that can be such a painful experience for contemplative people who long for intimacy with Christ but feel frustrated and disappointed when such intimacy is seemingly denied.

What then, he asks, can be the purpose of any further concealment? Bernard first quotes the Gospel assurance, 'Seek and you shall find',[27] and then Isaiah, 'Seek the LORD while he may be found'.[28] The bride, he is sure, could not be one of those unspiritual people to whom Christ said, 'You will seek me and you will not find me.'[29]

He goes on to suggest three possible reasons why those who seek are disappointed. They may be seeking at the wrong time, or in the wrong way, or in the wrong place. So he points out that Scripture itself implies this, in such sayings as 'Seek the LORD while he may be found', implying that there are times when he may not be found. He also refers to the parable of the foolish virgins who found the door to the wedding feast barred to them, and alludes to Christ's warning that 'the night is coming when no one can work'.[30]

Bernard is, of course, well aware that in this matter of the mystery of God's elusive presence he is dealing with something that is beyond human understanding. Yet God's absence is never to be seen as wholly negative, if the result is to increase human longing and to develop the graces of patience and perseverance.

In the same sermon, Bernard points out the significance of the phrase 'I sought him whom my soul loves':

> How beautifully then does the Bride speak when she says not 'him whom I love' but 'him whom my soul loves'.[31] For the love by which one loves spiritually . . . is truly and properly an attribute of the soul alone. Of this kind also is the love of justice, truth, goodness, wisdom, and the other virtues . . . So when the Bride says that her soul loves her Bridegroom, she uses an unusual expression, but one which is none the less appropriate, for it shows that the Bridegroom is a spirit, and that he is loved with a spiritual, not a physical, love.[32]

On the significance of the fact that it is night when the bride searched for her lover, Bernard, following a line of thought in St John's Gospel, tentatively suggests that 'night' stands for the darkness of the world which surrounds every lover of the Lord. And indeed, he says that not only the darkness of the world, its faithlessness, its ignorance, its perversity, but even 'the shameless and degraded behaviour of Catholics – these are all nights. For surely it is night when the things which belong to the Spirit of God are not perceived.' He goes on to deny that the bride would be so blind and foolish as now to seek him in the night. He notes, rather, the significance of the past tense ('I sought him'): by the night of darkness the poet means the ignorance of immaturity. She had looked for truth where it was not, wandering but not finding, straying like a lost sheep. Like St Augustine, she had been 'outside herself', as it were, and found God only when she found herself.

St Teresa of Avila (1515–82)

Like most religious women of her time, Teresa received no education in Holy Scripture. Yet despite the lack of formal training, and the limited access she had to the Bible, she was bold enough to write a short book, *Meditations on the Song of Songs*.

Following the Christian tradition in which she had been immersed, Teresa read the Song of Songs as a poetic allegory with a triple meaning: it could be read as being about the mutual love between Christ and his Church, between Christ and the Blessed Virgin Mary, or between Christ and the individual soul.

Teresa did not write her *Meditations* for the wider Church, but for the benefit of the sisters under her care. In the Prologue she tells her

sisters that even though she does not fully understand the meaning
of the Latin version, which was all that was available to her, 'my soul
is stirred and recollected more than by devotional books written
in the language I understand'. She continues: 'it seems to me that the
Lord has been giving me, for the sake of my purpose in writing this
work, some understanding of the meaning of certain words, and
I think these words will bring consolation to the Sisters our Lord
leads by this path and also to me.'[33]

For Teresa, the main obstacle to understanding Scripture was
not lack of learning, but sin, or lack of love for the Lord, and lack of
humility. She was critical of those who 'who can easily read the Song
of Songs every day and are not themselves involved with the words
[because they have no love]'.[34] It was not that Teresa thought that
her own spiritual experience was the best criterion for discerning
the meaning of Scripture; but as she pointed out, even the learned
biblical scholars, whom she took the trouble to consult, had written
many commentaries on the Song of Songs and had never finished
explaining the words. She observes that one word of the Lord's will
contain within it a thousand mysteries, and 'thus our understanding
is only very elementary'.

Teresa was always able to relate her teaching to her experience as
a spiritual director. So she writes:

> I know someone who for a number of years had many fears,
> and nothing gave her assurance, but the Lord was pleased that
> she heard some words from the Song of Songs, and through them
> she understood that her soul was well guided . . . she understood
> that it was possible for a soul in love with its Spouse to experience
> all those favours, swoons, deaths, afflictions, delights and joys
> in relation to Him. It does so after it has left all the world's joys
> out of love for Him, and is completely given over and abandoned
> into His hands, and . . . not just in words . . . but confirmed with
> deeds.[35]

Commenting on the first verse of the Song ('Let him kiss me with
the kisses of his mouth'[36]), Teresa prays to God:

> these words in themselves, taking them only literally, would truly
> cause fear if the one uttering them were in his senses. But the
> one whom you love, Lord, has drawn them out of himself. You

will truly pardon if he says them and also others, even though to say them is daring. And my Lord, if the kiss signifies peace and friendship why shouldn't souls ask you for this kiss? What better thing can we ask for than what I ask you for, my Lord; that you give me this peace 'with the kiss of your mouth'. This, daughters, is a lofty petition, as I shall tell you afterwards.[37]

Teresa was undoubtedly able to penetrate to the deepest content of biblical texts, especially when these texts related to what she knew most about – the inner life of the spirit. It is also evident that she read the Song not only as a comment on her own spiritual experience, but also within the framework of a wider ecclesial and indeed global context. She related the peace of Christ to the tangible and visible sacrament of the Eucharist, and wondered 'if the bride was asking for this favour that Christ afterward gave us'. She also wondered whether she was asking for that union so great that God became man, for that friendship that he effected with the human race. 'Obviously a kiss is the sign of great peace and friendship among two persons. May the Lord help us to understand how many kinds of peace there are.'[38]

In the third chapter, Teresa develops broader reflections on the same text. She believes that the holy peace which Christ alone can bring is one that requires a heroic willingness to venture out against all 'worldly forms of peace'. True peace and union with Christ are only possible when the Christian has brought her soul into union with the will of God. 'It is a union not based on words or desires alone, but a union proved by deeds.'[39] She gives many examples of what she means, all involving a total surrender of self-seeking motives. To desire that Christ, the Spouse, will 'kiss me with the kisses of his mouth' is understood as a desire that involves total commitment of intention. Through human weakness, that desire may sometimes lose its force, such that 'I may want to withdraw from this friendship and union [yet I still pray that] my will may always, Lord of my life, be subject to your will and not depart from it.'[40]

St John of the Cross (1542–91)

Juan de Yepes, or St John of the Cross, as he is more commonly known, was a younger contemporary of Teresa. He was chosen by her to be her Confessor and colleague in her project to reform the Carmelite Orders. John loved the Song of Songs. It was the chief inspiration behind *The Spiritual Canticle*, his great work of literary and spiritual art written while he was being kept in solitary confinement by a group of 'unreformed' Carmelites. John's spirituality is 'closest to that of the Song of Songs – ecstatic, erotic, sensual and loving'.[41] Intimacy with God is not to be gained by knowledge, but only by love. So it is that in mystical theology, 'strangeness', paradox and oddity are not only to be expected but welcomed. John understood mystical theology as being quite distinct from other types of theology in which the reason and intellect are supreme. He understood it as a form of discourse that subverts other forms of discourse, 'destabilizing "knowing" in a process of "unknowing", preferring experience or "taste" as a privileged location to engage with the living God'.[42] In this respect he followed a very similar tradition to that of the fourteenth-century English classic *The Cloud of Unknowing*.[43]

Three stanzas from the beginning of *The Spiritual Canticle* show how much John was inspired by the Song, especially by the theme of the wound suffered by the beloved:[44]

> Where have you hidden,
> My love, and left me moaning?
> Like a stag you fled
> Having wounded me;
> I went out calling you, and you had gone.
>
> And all who are free,
> Tell me a thousand graceful things of you;
> And all wound me more,
> And leave me dying:
> A-don't-know-what which lies behind their babbling.
>
> Why, if you wounded this heart
> Don't you heal it?
> And as you stole it from me,
> Why do you leave it as it is
> And not carry off what you have stolen?[45]

Part 2

TEXT, COMMENTARY AND REFLECTIONS

The title

1.1   The Song of Songs, which is Solomon's.

'Song of Songs' is Hebrew idiom for the superlative degree, so the meaning is: 'Solomon's Best Song'. Ancient tradition ascribed it to Solomon, but the language of the poem indicates that it came from a much later time.

As has already been suggested,[1] there is another possible connection with Solomon: a link with Solomon's greatest project – the Temple in Jerusalem. By the time the Song was accepted into the Hebrew Holy Scriptures, the Temple had been destroyed.[2] Thereafter, in different ways and for different reasons, both Jews and Christians were finding other less local and more universal means of access to God. A rabbinic story suggests that the Song of Songs was believed worthy to replace the Temple as a means of access to God.[3] The Song invites us to enter with loving prayer into the sacred place of our relationship with the beloved. The Song of Songs is not only Solomon's 'best song' but both 'God's best song' and 'Our best song to God'.

> We read the Song IN CHRIST. Christ is in our midst singing his Song of Songs. He is at the centre, and ever shall be singing his Canticle of Love . . . Christ knocks at the door of your heart, saying Come within, and see.[4]

The invitation to enter the Song with loving prayer must also include reflecting on the meaning of suffering: 'the wound of love', which we shall encounter later.[5]

> My song is love unknown,
> My Saviour's love to me;
> Love to the loveless shown,
> That they might lovely be.
> O who am I,
> That for my sake
> My Lord should take
> Frail flesh, and die?
>   Samuel Crossman (1624–83)[6]

ೞೞೞೞೞೞ ☼ ೫೫೫೫೫೫

Longing for love

> 1.2 Let him kiss me with the kisses of his mouth!
> For your love is better than wine.
> 1.3 your anointing oils are fragrant,
> your name is perfume poured out:
> therefore the maidens love you.
> 1.4 Draw me after you, let us make haste.
> The king has brought me into his chambers.
> We will exult and rejoice in you;
> we will extol your love more than wine;
> rightly do they love you.

As the poem opens we are immediately caught up into the action, but are we overhearing a conversation or is it a soliloquy? And there is a puzzling series of disconnections in the personal pronouns and nouns: *him – me – your – your – your – me – us – me – you – we – they – you*. Do 'him' and 'you' and 'your' all refer to 'the king'? Who are included in 'we'? The language is like the transcription of a dream, in which images and people are confused. Is this an example of the incongruous language to which the third-century biblical scholar Origen referred when he stated that the anomalous language of the Song indicates that the poem is best read not literally but allegorically?[1]

What is most striking here is the woman's powerful expression of her desire for her lover. Her intense longing dominates the whole poem. In fact it is this heart-felt yearning, rather than finding fulfilment, which provides a clue to the nature of the Song.

The next thing to notice in these lines is their highly sensuous quality, evoking the senses of sight and taste and smell. In this poem all three senses are significant but here the sense of sweet smell is most important: 'fragrant' anointing oil, and 'your name is perfume poured out'. To the first readers of this poem sweet smells would quite likely have brought to mind a royal banquet scene. Fragrant anointing oil would also suggest the oil mixed with balsam with which the high priest or the king was anointed.

Here is a possible clue to the character of this poem. Is it one in which the hope of a Messiah may be found? Fragrant anointing oil is part of the gospel story, and symbolizes both passionate love and death. One of the gifts brought by the magi to the infant Jesus was myrrh, an ointment used in preparing a body for burial.

We also recall the story of Mary of Bethany who anointed Jesus' feet with costly nard, and as a result of her extravagant action 'the house was filled with the fragrance of the perfume'.[2]

At one level, these fragrant oils and perfumes have obvious associations with human love-making. But at another they are important for certain kinds of religious experience. The warm and fragrant smell of smoking frankincense is an outward sign of prayer going up to heaven. The sense of smell goes very deep. Sights and sounds sometimes distract us, but a characteristic or memorable scent brings to mind things we thought we had forgotten. Do we perhaps find that the deliberate emphasis on fragrant smells in these opening verses draws us into an ambience conducive to contemplative prayer?

ઝઝઝઝઝઝ ✿ ଔଔଔଔଔଔ

ઝ *3* ઝ

Kiss me

1.2   Let him kiss me with the kisses of his mouth!

As some of the early rabbis pointed out, the phrase 'kisses of his mouth' is a strange one. Would not 'kisses of his lips' be more typical if this were a straightforward expression of physical desire? In the Hebrew Scriptures the mouth is more often associated with speaking than with kissing, so the rabbis understood the term 'kisses' as metaphorical rather than literal, meaning an intimate greeting or touching. The 'mouth of the Lord' is a very common phrase throughout the Old Testament, especially in the prophetical books, and it usually implies a definitive speech of God: 'The mouth of the LORD has spoken it.'[1] So when in the first century CE the Jewish rabbis first published commentaries on the Song of Songs, they took this verse as the key to the whole poem, reading it as an allegory of God's relationship with Israel. This opened the way for Christian writers and preachers to reapply the metaphor in the light of the Incarnation, and so to interpret the Song as an allegory about Christ's relationship with the Church, the new Israel.[2] According to one Christian interpretation, the bride Israel received the kiss she longed for when Jesus was born in Bethlehem, for it was then that the Word of God became flesh and blood, and the divine Lover became fully and physically present in Israel.

The relationship between the divine Lover and the individual beloved soul has a long and rich history, as we have already seen exemplified in the Christian tradition from Origen to St John of the Cross.[3] The Welsh poet Ann Griffiths was a farmer's wife without any formal education but in her short life she was greatly influenced by the Methodist Revival. She died in 1805 'leaving a handful of hymns still remarkable for their bold and extravagant imagery and sustained emotional density'.[4] The verse below boldly illustrates her personal experience of Christ's power to redeem through his death and Passion, thus restoring God's image that was lost. The theme of the divine Lover in the Song of Songs was central to her spirituality.

Hymn for the Mercy Seat
I shall lift up the name that God
Sets out to be a mercy seat, a healing and the veils,
And the imaginings and shrouds have gone, because
My soul stands now, his finished likeness,
Admitted now to share his secret, that his blood and hurt
Showed once, now I shall kiss the Son
And never turn away again. And never
Turn away.

Ann Griffiths (1776–1805)

The experience of being 'kissed', 'touched' or 'looked upon' by God at some point in one's early life, as a child or a youth, is quite a common one. The seventeenth-century English poet George Herbert expressed his sense of having been glanced at by God's 'sweet and gracious eye', and feeling a 'sug'red strange delight'. Paradoxically, this sense of being looked at occurred not when he felt close to God, but after a time of youthful estrangement from God. The experience left its mark on him, and made him conscious of God's love and protection through troubled times, and ignited his yearning hope and desire that one day he would be enveloped in God's blazing light and see God face to face.

The Glance

When first thy sweet and gracious eye
Vouchsaf'd ev'n in the midst of youth and night
To look upon me, who before did lie
    Weltring in sin;
  I felt a sug'red strange delight,
Passing all cordials made by any art,
Bedew, embalm, and overrun my heart,
    And take it in.

Since that time many a bitter storm
My soul hath felt, ev'n able to destroy,
Had the malicious and ill-meaning harm
    His swing and sway:
  But still thy sweet original joy,
Sprung from thine eye, did work within my soul,
And surging griefs, when they grew bold, control,
    And got the day.

If thy first glance so powerful be,
A mirth but open'd and seal'd up again;
What wonders shall we feel, when we shall see
    Thy full-ey'd love!
  When thou shalt look us out of pain,
And one aspect of thine spend in delight
More than a thousand suns disburse in light,
    In heav'n above.

ଔଔଔଔଔଔ ☼ ଯଯଯଯଯଯ

ଔ4ଔ

Loving intimacy

1.4   Draw me after you, let us make haste.
        The king has brought me into his chambers.
    We will exult and rejoice in you;
        we will extol your love more than wine;
        rightly do they love you.

The phrase 'draw me' recalls the beautiful line in Hosea: 'I drew them [Israel] with the bands of love'; and in Jeremiah: 'I have loved you (Israel) with an everlasting love, therefore I drew you with constancy.'[1] 'The king has brought me into his chambers', that is, the place of loving intimacy with the Lord.

Another clue about the deeper meaning of this poem may be found in the words: 'We will exult and rejoice in you; we will extol your love more than wine.' This verse suggests a purposeful commitment to remember the beloved with intense joy. Also, the words 'we will exult and rejoice in you' stand out as a phrase that is too elevated for ordinary love poetry. Moreover, as the word 'we' is plural, not singular, the woman is here not alone, but speaks for a group or community. The phrase sounds as if it were from a religious tradition – like a psalm. In fact, we meet similar words in Psalm 118.24, often sung at a corporate celebration such as Passover or Easter. 'This is the day that the LORD has made; let us rejoice and be glad in it.' So while these lines are in one respect intensely personal, they also suggest a public celebration such as a wedding, one in which the woman shares with others the joy of her love.

These reflections should confirm our already strong impression that this poem has not just one meaning, but rather many meanings. But in order to see this more clearly, we need to explore the Song further, and in particular to note what kind of associations its language would have both for its original audience, and for later Christian readers.

ᚒᚒᚒᚒᚒᚒ ☼ ᚒᚒᚒᚒᚒᚒ

ᚒ 5 ᚒ

Black and beautiful

1.5 I am black and beautiful,
   O daughters of Jerusalem;
  like the tents of Kedar,
   like the curtains of Solomon.
1.6 Do not gaze at me because I am dark,
   because the sun has gazed on me.

My mother's sons were angry with me;
they made me keeper of the vineyards,
but my own I have not kept!

The theme of blackness permeates these verses: not just the physical swarthiness of the woman's skin caused by labouring in the harsh Middle Eastern sun, but also emotionally – the black depression of one who felt herself rejected by her own 'mother's sons'. In other scriptural texts, blackness of skin is associated with suffering, both physical and mental.[1] Not only did her brothers' unkind action bring her more work, but this extra burden was put on her by the very people who by ties of kinship might have been expected to give her the most support.

The tents of Kedar to which the woman compares herself were black because they were woven from the wool of black goats. In the Psalms, the tents of Kedar are associated with the mental suffering caused by feelings of estrangement, or sin: 'Woe is me that . . . I must live among the tents of Kedar.'[2] In contrast to the blackness of the tents of Kedar, the curtains of Solomon, which hung before the Holy of Holies in the Temple, were woven of fine linen with blue, purple and crimson threads and embroidered with representations of the cherubim.[3] As such they were the image of refinement and beauty.

So although the woman feels herself to be darkened by the sun, and distressed by her brothers' rejection, she is nevertheless aware that she is still 'beautiful'. She has not lost her youthful beauty.

At a literal level, we seem to have here just the briefest hint of a story, but no reason is given for the brothers' anger, and they reappear only at the end of the poem, where they are heard scorning their 'little sister'.[4] We are bound to look deeper. Is this black but beautiful woman a symbol of suffering love?

There are said to be more than 450 Black Madonnas in Europe, some of the most famous being at Montserrat near Barcelona, Czestochowa in Poland and Guingamp in Brittany. France is home to at least 180, nearly all of them dating from the eleventh to the fifteenth centuries. They are mostly made of wood, but occasionally of stone, often painted and up to 75 centimetres tall. Their connection with these verses of the Song is not proven, but such a reference seems quite possible in view of the growing cult of the Virgin Mary during the Middle Ages when the Song reached the height of popularity.

These verses may thus lead us to meditating on Mary's role in the salvation of the world, Mary herself being the perfect icon of contemplative prayer, the one who 'treasured all these things in her heart'.[5]

This twenty-first-century version of Mary's song Magnificat[6] draws out the themes of thankfulness and humility, and the centrality of love that 'goes deeper than human thinking', taking us into silent prayer.

> My soul sings in gratitude.
> I'm dancing in the mystery of God.
> The light of the Holy One is within me
> and I am blessed, so truly blessed.
>
> This goes deeper than human thinking.
> I am filled with awe
> at Love whose only condition
> is to be received.
>
> The gift is not for the proud,
> for they have no room for it.
> The strong and self-sufficient ones
> don't have this awareness.
>
> But those who know their emptiness
> can rejoice in Love's fullness.
>
> It's the Love that we are made for,
> the reason for our being.
>
> It fills our inmost heart space
> and brings to birth in us, the Holy One.
>   Joy Cowley (b. 1936), New Zealand

CR CR CR CR CR CR CR ☼ RC RC RC RC RC RC

CR 6 CR

Black and beautiful – Jerusalem

Another way of reading these verses is to identify the female speaker as the city of Jerusalem and her Temple. The confession of her 'blackness' may thus be an acknowledgement of Israel's rebellion against God. In the major Prophets, especially Jeremiah and Lamentations, Jerusalem is personified as a sinful woman and frequently reminded by the prophet of her sins: 'Only acknowledge your guilt, that you have rebelled against the Lord your God';[1] 'Jerusalem sinned grievously, so she has become a mockery.'[2] Jesus, too, speaks more than once with anguish of the tragedy of Jerusalem:

> Jerusalem, Jerusalem, the city that kills the prophets and stones those that are sent to it! How often have I desired to gather your children together as a hen gathers her brood under her wings, and you were not willing![3]

Jerusalem is beautiful because it is the place in which God's glory dwells, but the arrogance, corruption and moral turpitude of its rulers had made it a place of sin. Its tragic destruction so soon after his Passion and death was, it seems, inevitable.

That Jerusalem is both sinful and yet still beautiful fits well with the prophetic message, which is not only one of condemnation but one of mercy. 'Return, faithless Israel', says the Lord, 'I will not look on you in anger, for I am merciful.'[4] 'I will give you shepherds after my own heart who will feed you with knowledge and understanding.'[5] Faithless Jerusalem, standing for Israel as a whole, can yet hope that despite all her sins God will still act on her behalf to bring about her salvation. So St Paul was sure that his fellow countrymen, despite their rejection of Jesus and his gospel, had continued to be God's beloved, and would receive God's mercy: 'For the gifts and the calling of God are irrevocable.'[6]

Holy places of pilgrimage may be at the same time beautiful and yet deeply infected by human pride and sin. For many years the Church of the Holy Sepulchre (Resurrection) in modern Jerusalem, visited by thousands of Christian pilgrims every year, has been a focus for unseemly strife between different Christian denominations who share ownership. The only person who can be trusted with the key is a Muslim. Religious movements start out with the highest ideals, but too often become battlegrounds of competing aspirations in which anger and frustrations may boil over into intemperate words and behaviour. No one who has been a member of a church for very long will be unaware of this. It is something that brings shame and necessary penitence for the sin and folly in which we all take a share.

Have mercy on me, O God,
  according to your steadfast love;
according to your abundant mercy
  blot out my transgressions.
Wash me thoroughly from my iniquity,
  and cleanse me from my sin.
For I know my transgressions,
  and my sin is ever before me.
Against you, you alone, have I sinned,
  and done what is evil in your sight . . .

Purge me with hyssop, and I shall be clean;
  wash me, and I shall be whiter than snow . . .
Hide your face from my sins,
  and blot out all my iniquities

Create in me a clean heart, O God,
  and put a new and right spirit within me.
Do not cast me away from your presence,
  and do not take your holy spirit from me.
Restore to me the joy of your salvation,
  and sustain in me a willing spirit.[7]

ෆෆෆෆෆෆ ✿ ෩෩෩෩෩෩

ෆ 7 ෆ

Black and beautiful – God's wisdom

The terms 'black and beautiful' may also be read as describing God's Wisdom. As has already been shown, God's Wisdom is frequently personified in the later Jewish Scriptures as a quasi-divine being: female, pure and beautiful.[1]

For she [Wisdom] is a breath of the power of God,
  and a pure emanation of the glory of the Almighty;
therefore nothing defiled gains entrance into her.
For she is a reflection of eternal light,
  a spotless mirror of the working of God,

and an image of his goodness . . .
She is more beautiful than the sun,
and excels every constellation of the stars.[2]

Wisdom is praised by the author of the Wisdom of Solomon as if
she were a choice partner, the best of companions, the perfect 'wife'.

Therefore I determined to take her to live with me,
knowing that she would give me good counsel
and encouragement in cares and grief.[3]

Now comparing this passage with the Song, we find an obvious parallel.
Here the woman is the adored and lovely companion, seen as beauty
itself, 'comely as Jerusalem'.

You are beautiful as Tirzah, my love,
comely as Jerusalem.[4]

If the woman of the Song is comparable in her beauty to Jerusalem,
then as the perfect 'wife' she also represents Divine Wisdom. Here
our thoughts may well turn from the historical Jerusalem, described
by St Paul as now 'in slavery with her children', to the 'Jerusalem
above; she is free, and she is our mother'. The heavenly city, which is
free and our mother, is portrayed by St John the Divine as 'the new
Jerusalem, coming down out of heaven from God, prepared as a bride
adorned for her husband'.[5] Here is the fulfilment of all human history, when Christ who is the Alpha and the Omega, the beginning
and the end, brings all things to a victorious close:

And I heard a loud voice from the throne saying,
'See, the home of God is among mortals.
He will dwell with them;
they will be his peoples,
and God himself will be with them;
he will wipe every tear from their eyes.
Death will be no more;
mourning and crying and pain will be no more,
for the first things have passed away.'
And the one who was seated on the throne said,
'See I am making all things new.'[6]

ೞೞೞೞೞೞ ✿ ೞೞೞೞೞೞ

ೞ8ೞ

Black and beautiful – The darkness of God

The beauty of God's wisdom may appear indeed more beautiful than the sun, yet there is also in God a 'darkness' of the unknowable and incomprehensible. God's wisdom, as Paul teaches, is not like human wisdom:

> Has not God made foolish the wisdom of the world? For since in the wisdom of God, the world did not know God through wisdom . . . For Jews demand signs and Greeks desire wisdom, but we proclaim Christ crucified . . . Christ the power of God and the wisdom of God. For God's foolishness is wiser than human wisdom.[1]

God's wisdom is proclaimed as 'Christ crucified, a stumbling block to Jews and foolishness to Gentiles'. Yet for many today the cross is not a source of consolation – the supreme example of God's love – but an obstacle to belief. They ask: how could God let his Messiah undergo such suffering and such a cruel death? They have not yet understood the good news that God's love is so powerful that it can overcome the worst that human beings can do to one another, and the greatest suffering that can be borne. Ultimately, however, God's wisdom is beyond the scope of our human rationality, just as God's essential being is to be found beyond all human images, ideas and thought.

As the mystics attest, God's wisdom is indeed to be found in darkness and mystery. Here is the 'dazzling darkness', the God who is ineffable, and indescribable, the God of the *via negativa* which so fascinated the sixth-century philosopher and theologian Dionysius,[2] and his disciple, the fourteenth-century anonymous author of *The Cloud of Unknowing*. Infinitely beyond all language and words, this dark mystery of God also inspired the seventeenth-century priest Henry Vaughan to write his poem 'The Night'.

> **The Night**
> Through that pure Virgin-shrine,
> That sacred veil drawn o'er thy glorious noon
> That men might look and live as glow-worms shine,
> And face the moon:

Wise Nicodemus saw such light
As made him know his God by night.

Most blest believer he!
Who in that land of darkness and blind eyes
Thy long expected healing wings could see,
    When thou didst rise,
    And what can never more be done,
    Did at mid-night speak with the Sun!

O who will tell me, where
He found thee at that dead and silent hour!
What hallowed solitary ground did bear
    So rare a flower,
    Within whose sacred leaves did lie
    The fullness of the Deity.

No mercy-seat of gold,
No dead and dusty Cherub, nor carved stone,
But his own living works did my Lord hold
    And lodge alone;
    Where trees and herbs did watch and peep
    And wonder, while the Jews did sleep.

Dear night! this world's defeat;
The stop to busy fools; care's check and curb;
The day of Spirits; my soul's calm retreat
    Which none disturb!
    Christ's progress, and his prayer time;
    The hours to which high Heaven doth chime.

God's silent, searching flight:
When my Lord's head is filled with dew, and all
His locks are wet with the clear drops of night;
    His still, soft call;
    His knocking time; the soul's dumb watch,
    When Spirits their fair kindred catch.

Were all my loud, evil days
Calm and unhaunted as is thy dark Tent,
Whose peace but by some Angel's wing or voice
    Is seldom rent;

Then I in Heaven all the long year
Would keep, and never wander here.

But living where the sun
Doth all things wake, and where all mix and tire
Themselves and others, I consent and run
To every mire,
And by this world's ill-guiding light,
Err more than I can do by night.

There is in God (some say)
A deep, but dazzling darkness; as men here
Say it is late and dusky, because they
See not all clear;
O for that night! Where I in him
Might live invisible and dim.

ෆෆෆෆෆෆෆ ☼ ෨෨෨෨෨෨

ෆ 9 ෆ

Dialogue

(Woman)
1.7   Tell me, you whom my soul loves,
     where you pasture your flock,
     where you make it lie down at noon;
  for why should I be like one who is veiled
     beside the flocks of your companions?
(Man)
1.8   If you do not know,
     O fairest among women,
  follow the tracks of the flock,
     and pasture your kids
     beside the shepherds' tents.

Here we are given a glimpse of a new scene – a pastoral setting, where the woman and the man each have flocks to tend. There is a dialogue between them about the care of their respective flocks. The woman addresses the man as 'you whom my soul loves'. We meet this unusual expression several times in the poem, especially in chapter 3. Here there appears to be some anxiety in the woman's question. She seems to be seeking peace and security, and she receives reassurance from her Lover.

Who are 'your companions'? They – 'my companions' – are referred to again almost at the end of the poem.[1] There they dwell in the gardens with the gardener, and hear his voice. If the shepherds' tents are the dwelling place of God, as in the Psalms,[2] then the shepherds are the human guardians of the flock. According to the prophets Jeremiah and Ezekiel,[3] the shepherds – that is, the religious and civic leaders of Israel – wretchedly failed in their calling by feeding themselves and neglecting their sheep. Here in the Song the reverse is true. The shepherds are fulfilling their role in harmony with the Chief Shepherd, the Shepherd of Israel. They are prefiguring Christ, the Good Shepherd of the sheep, who will gather into one fold all those called by him.[4]

The role of shepherd or pastor is one that is central to the life of every Christian community. Surprisingly perhaps, the earliest pictures of Christ, found in the catacombs in Rome and dating back to the times of persecution, do not portray the Lord's crucifixion or resurrection. They depict Jesus in the classical image of a shepherd who pastures and tends his flock. The picture of a shepherd who gives his life for the sheep in his care is a natural development of this image, and was immortalized in St John's Gospel. Jesus said: 'I am the good shepherd. The good shepherd lays down his life for the sheep.'[5]

CS CS CS CS CS CS ✿ EO EO EO EO EO EO

CS 10 CS

The language of mutual love

1.9   I compare you, my love,
        To a mare among Pharaoh's chariots.

1.10   Your cheeks are comely with ornaments,
        your neck with strings of jewels.

1.11   We will make you ornaments of gold,
        studded with silver.

Here it makes good sense to follow the Jewish Targum – that is, the Aramaic translation of, and commentary on, the original Hebrew text. The word for 'circlets' is interpreted as meaning the Torah (Law) in both its written and oral forms, and could be readily related to Psalm 19, where the psalmist speaks of the ordinances of God as 'more to be desired are they than gold, even much fine gold'.[1] Likewise, 'studs of silver' relate to Psalm 12: 'The promises of the LORD are promises that are pure, silver refined in a furnace ... purified seven times.'[2] The Targum comments that 'gold' stands for the inner sense of the Torah, while 'silver' for the outer sense. The meaning of these three verses then, taken together, could be that the woman or bride, under the metaphor of the female horse, arrayed in splendid trappings and jewellery, is being portrayed as gloriously clothed in God's Law and commandments. She is Israel herself. 'The law of the LORD is perfect, reviving the soul; the decrees of the LORD are sure, making wise the simple; the precepts of the LORD are right, rejoicing the heart.'[3]

> Happy are those whose way is blameless,
>   who walk in the law of the LORD ...
> Lead me in the path of your commandments,
>   for I delight in it ...
> See, I have longed for your precepts;
>   in your righteousness give me life.[4]

There is no indication anywhere in the Old Testament that *Torah* (that is, law) in any of its meanings or uses is perceived as anything other than a good thing. And that is the problem when it is translated as 'Law', especially with the capital letter, because in much influential Christian use 'Law' has a bad name. It is not going too far to say that in Judaism 'Torah' (Law) stands for the good news of God ... and for which the English term 'gospel' would not be an inappropriate translation.[5]

ᴄꙅᴄꙅᴄꙅᴄꙅᴄꙅᴄꙅ ☼ ᴆᴑᴆᴑᴆᴑᴆᴑᴆᴑᴆᴑ

ᴄꙅ *11* ᴄꙅ

Fragrant nard

> 1.12   While the king was on his couch,
>   my nard gave forth its fragrance.

The word 'king' occurs four times in the Song, twice in connection with Solomon. Frequent and sudden changes of image occur throughout the Song. Is the king here a royal figure or a divine one? God is the first and ultimate king of Israel. For Christians, there is only one who is King of kings and Lord of lords: the risen and ascended Christ, whose table is that of the heavenly banquet foreshadowed in the sacramental and earthly Eucharist. Here, picking up on the reference to anointing oils in 1.3, we explore the meaning of the fragrance of nard in the context of the Gospels.

> While Jesus was at Bethany in the house of Simon the leper, as he sat at table, a woman came with an alabaster jar of very costly ointment of nard, and she broke open the jar and poured the ointment on his head.[1]

In all four Gospels the poignant story is told of Jesus and the woman who anointed his feet. Mark's version, quoted above, goes on to tell how some of the company strongly objected to the action, suggesting that the ointment could have been sold for 300 denarii (the equivalent of 300 people's day-wage in today's money), and the money given to the poor.

At one level this deed could be understood as an act of devotion to Jesus (as is the case in Luke). But Jesus' words in response to her action draw our attention to his imminent death and subsequent burial.

> Jesus said, 'Let her alone; why do you trouble her? ... For you always have the poor with you, and you can show kindness to them whenever you wish; but you will not always have me. She has done what she could; she has anointed my body beforehand for its burial. Truly I tell you, wherever the good news is proclaimed in the whole world, what she has done will be told in remembrance of her.'[2]

In the other three Gospels, details of the story are a little different.[3] In Matthew it is the disciples, not others, who object to the woman's action, and 'nard' is not mentioned. In Luke the point of the story is that the woman is a well-known sinner, and the woman's action is her loving response to the fact that she has been forgiven. In John the incident occurs in Bethany in the home of Martha and Mary, the house where Jesus is staying, and where he has just raised their brother Lazarus from the dead. It is Mary herself who takes a pound of pure nard to anoint Jesus' feet, which she then wipes with her hair, and 'the house was filled with the fragrance of the perfume'. The one who protests here is Judas Iscariot. Jesus responds in words very similar to those recorded in Mark. 'Leave her alone. She bought it so that she might keep it for the day of my burial. You always have the poor with you, but you do not always have me.'[4]

The substance 'nard' in the Gospels, like 'myrrh', is not just an ointment suitable for anointing a dead body. Because of its costliness, it is pre-eminently appropriate for a king and one who has already been, metaphorically, anointed by God: that is, the messiah ('anointed one').

As already noted, 'fragrance' is a key word in the Song,[5] occurring no fewer than eight times. It also often recurs in the Christian tradition in connection with prayer, especially the interior prayer of the saints and mystics. In the words of John Cassian, whose writings on the prayers of the Desert Fathers were to have such a great influence on Christian teaching in both West and East:

> Often by the sudden visitation of God, we are filled with perfumes sweeter than any made by man, so that the soul is enraptured with delight and, as it were, caught up into an ecstasy of spirit, becoming unconscious that it still dwells in the flesh.[6]

St Teresa of Avila also speaks in similar, even more graphic terms, of the fragrance to be found in her experience of prayer of the heart:

> The whole creature, both body and soul, is enraptured as if some very fragrant ointment, resembling a delicious perfume, had been infused into the very centre of the being [marrow], or as if we had suddenly entered a place redolent with scents coming not from one, but from many objects; we do not know from which it arises nor what it is, although it entirely pervades our being.[7]

ങ‍ങ‍ങ‍ങ‍ങ‍ങ ☼ ഗ‍ഗ‍ഗ‍ഗ‍ഗ‍ഗ

ങ *12* ഗ

Ecstatic love

1.13   My beloved is to me a bag of myrrh
that lies between my breasts.

1.14 My beloved is to me a cluster of henna blossoms
      in the vineyards of En-gedi.

1.15 Ah, you are beautiful, my love;
      Ah, you are beautiful;
      your eyes are doves.

1.16 Ah, you are beautiful, my beloved,
      truly lovely.
      Our couch is green;

1.17 the beams of our house are cedar,
      our rafters are pine.

The poem rises to its first climax of ecstatic love, in which both male and female express their love in terms of complete equality. They almost seem to be competing with each other in their expressions of love and delight. The words 'Ah, you are beautiful' are spoken at first by the man, and then echoed by the woman. But the words translated 'my love' and 'my beloved' do not quite convey the meaning of the original. The man most often calls his beloved '*ra'yati*', which means 'comrade/friend' or 'mate'. The word implies equality. She calls him '*dodi*': my darling, my lover. Throughout the whole poem the woman appears as someone who is beautiful, but also strong, even dauntingly attractive: 'formidable' (in the French sense).

Erotic love and mystical love

The close connection between the language of human erotic love and that of the mystic was discussed in Chapter 2. In 1955 Dom Bede Griffiths was sent to South India by his Benedictine community in England.[1] In Tamil Nadu he helped to establish a Christian community in a traditional Indian 'ashram' setting called Shantivanam. In his words, 'In India I found the other half of my soul.' There he developed a Christ-centred mysticism: 'It is no accident that the mystical experience is sometimes described in terms of sexual union. This is not a sublimation in the Freudian sense. Rather it is an opening of human nature to the full dimension of its being.'[2] Towards the end of his life, he spoke more profoundly of the relationship between sexual and mystical experience. Drawing on his knowledge of the writings of the poet and novelist D. H. Lawrence, he stated his belief that Lawrence, through his experience of sex, had come to a genuine

59

experience of transcendental reality.³ Bede referred to these words from Lawrence's *Women in Love*:

> How can I say I love you when I have ceased to be? We are both caught up and transcended into a new awareness where everything is silent because there is nothing to answer. All is perfect and at one. Speech travels between separate parts but in the perfect one there is perfect silence of bliss.⁴

Griffiths himself had come to this firm conviction:

> in the Mystical Body of Christ which embraces all redeemed humanity, we do not disappear in the Godhead but we discover a personal relationship of love. Each person is fulfilled and open to the other person; it is an inter-communion of love in which each embraces the other and all are embraced by God.⁵

ೞೞೞೞೞೞ ☼ ಬಬಬಬಬಬ

ೞ *13* ೞ

The flowering of love

> 2.1 I am a rose of Sharon,
> a lily of the valleys.
>
> 2.2 As a lily among the brambles,
> so is my love among maidens.

In the prophets Isaiah and Hosea, roses and lilies are both symbols of the beauty of Jerusalem, or Israel, restored after a time of estrangement from God, and destruction by their enemies. Thus Isaiah says: 'The wilderness and the dry land shall be glad, and the desert shall rejoice and blossom; like the crocus it shall blossom abundantly.'¹ And Hosea proclaims God's love: 'I will love them freely . . . I will be like the dew to Israel; he shall blossom like the lily. They shall again live beneath my shadow . . . they shall blossom like the vine, and their fragrance shall be like the wine of Lebanon.'²

Almost every word in these lines from Hosea is echoed in the Song. It seems as if God's promise of 'freely given love' is being fulfilled, when the woman 'lives beneath God's shadow'. It is as if God is bringing back Israel, and through Israel the whole of humanity, to the paradisal state of Eden. The flowers are symbols both of divine *eros*, the passion of God, and of his forgiving and self-giving love, in which God restores his people to a covenant relationship based on God's faithful promises.

The blooming of Israel's desert landscape is a metaphor of God's faithfulness and a celebration of love. The lovers see the land of Israel in its fullest bloom. And in addition, it is fragrant with perfumes and scents of distant lands.

Moreover, the woman herself is depicted as 'a lily among brambles'. A medieval tradition identifies the rose and the lily with the Virgin Mary and this is celebrated in songs such as the fifteenth-century German hymn 'Es ist ein' Ros' entsprungen':

> There is a flower springing
> From tender roots it grows,
> From Eden beauty bringing
> From Jesse's stem a rose
> On his green branch it blows;
> A bud that in cold winter
> At midnight will unclose.
>
> Pure Mary, maiden holy,
> The dream by prophets seen,
> Who in a stable lowly
> Above her child did lean
> So gentle and serene:
> This was Esaias' vision,
> The tree of living green.
>
> To Mary, rose of heaven,
> With loving hearts we say
> Let our sins be forgiven,
> And grief be turned away
> Upon this Christmas Day;
> To Jesus, child of winter,
> For grace and hope we pray.[3]

∽ 14 ∽

The apple tree

> 2.3 As an apple tree among the trees of the wood,
> so is my beloved among young men.
> With great delight I sat in his shadow,
> and his fruit was sweet to my taste.

Because of its tasty and nutritious fruit, the apple tree can be counted as superior to all other trees of the wood. So, too, the beloved sees her lover as superior to all other rivals. This metaphor may have its roots in the fertile land of what is now southern Iraq. In one nuptial poem from the ancient Sumerian people of southern Mesopotamia, the bride refers to her bridegroom as 'My apple-tree that bears fruit up to its crown'.[1]

While the apple is indeed an ancient symbol for love, the mystics would interpret this love as the love of God that attracts a person to prayer, to the experience of dwelling in the shade of God's spirit, and of tasting the sweetness of the fruit of the Spirit: love, joy, peace, patience, kindness, generosity, faithfulness, gentleness and self-control.[2]

∽∽∽∽∽∽ ☼ ∾∾∾∾∾∾

∽ 15 ∽

The banqueting house

> 2.4 He brought me to the banqueting house,
> and his intention towards me was love.
> 2. 5 Sustain me with raisins,
> refresh me with apples . . .

The reference to raisins as well as apples is significant here. The poet may be wanting to remind his readers of the story of the bringing of the sacred ark of the Tabernacle into Jerusalem. It is a story that revealed the young King David as a fearless man who was not shy of showing his religious fervour by a display of wild leaping and dancing.

> As the ark of the LORD came into the city of David, Michal daughter of Saul looked out of the window, and saw King David leaping and dancing before the LORD; and she despised him in her heart.[1]

The arrival of the ark of the Lord in Jerusalem was followed by the king himself making a series of offerings to the Lord. David then blessed the people, and distributed food to them, including 'raisin cakes'.

It seems that the poet here may be wishing to highlight the historic beginnings of David's reign and the arrival of the holy ark of the Lord's presence into Jerusalem. From that moment Zion became a city holy to the Lord, an event that prepared the way for the building of the first Temple, under King Solomon.

The royal 'banqueting house' is an apt composite symbol for the place both of eucharistic worship and of the final wedding feast of the Lamb: 'And the angel said to me, "Write this: Blessed are those who are invited to the marriage supper of the Lamb."'[2]

So here in the Song is another fascinating hint of God's near presence – sweet nourishing food, manna from heaven, a foretaste of the heavenly banquet, a sign of his grace and love.

> God, the source of all holiness
> and giver of all good things:
> may we who have shared at this table
> as strangers and pilgrims here on earth
> be welcomed with all your saints
> to the heavenly feast on the day of your kingdom.[3]

16

The wound of love (1)

2.5 . . . for I am faint with love.

Origen's reading of this phrase was based on the Greek translation of the Hebrew, where it reads: 'I am wounded by love.'[1] Although this was a mistaken translation, Origen's interpretation had the merit of leading readers to realize that the love being referred to may be something different from the emotions of someone smitten by an earthly love affair. In his commentary Origen wrote:

> The soul is moved by heavenly love and longing when, having clearly beheld the beauty and the fairness of the Word of God, it falls deeply in love with His loveliness and receives from the Word himself a certain dart and wound of love.[2]

The theme of 'the wound of love' or 'holy wound' recurs throughout the later centuries among writers in the mystical tradition, as was discussed in Chapter 4. The quotation there from the *Spiritual Canticle* of St John of the Cross shows that he was deeply influenced by his reading of the Song of Songs. There will be more on this theme when we come to the Song 5.8.

The 'wound of love' refers to the anguish that people of prayer feel when the Lord they seek to love seems not only absent or inaccessible, but at times deliberately avoiding their approach. We have already heard St Teresa's complaint, that when in the midst of her busy life she puts time aside to enter into contemplative prayer God fails to be present for her. Teresa accuses God of not caring: in effect, of deliberate cruelty. If that is true for her, it must be true for others. This is one aspect of the wound of love.

Some of the Psalms of lament seem to spring from that same wounded place in the heart, caused by God's apparent absence or neglect. The theme of God hiding himself, or God's unwillingness to listen, finds expression in these lines:

> 'How long, O LORD? Will you forget me for ever:
> How long will you hide your face from me?'[3]

> 'O my God, I cry by day, but you do not answer;
> and by night, but find no rest.'[4]

> 'But I, O LORD, cry out to you;
> in the morning my prayer comes before you.
> O LORD, why do you cast me off?
> Why do you hide your face from me?'[5]

CBCBCBCBCBCB ☼ ꝏꝏꝏꝏꝏꝏ

☙ 17 ❧

The wound of love (2)

> 2.5   . . . for I am faint with love.

A sense of personal or collective failure and disappointment are common enough. But if we remain firmly locked within our own pain and disenchantment, that choice leads to diminishment of vitality, and a loss of purpose and direction. On the other hand, if we can but perceive these times of desolation as the 'wounds of God's love', they become channels of God's grace – instruments of expansion of spirit, drawing us into a deeper relationship with God and into a greater solidarity with others, not least those whose lot is more painful than ours.

The Celtic Christian story of the Fisher King, originating in the Arthurian legend of the Holy Grail, is of special interest here. As a young man the Fisher King receives a mysterious wound while hunting in the forest, which does not heal and which causes his kingdom to suffer too – the whole Grail Castle and its lands fester and wither away. According to one contemporary psychologist, this mysterious wound can be seen as a symbol of the first transcendent experience many young people go through; but, being young, they are unable to cope with it or integrate it into their lives. So most Western people are Fisher Kings who have blundered into something too big for them. 'As a result they drop it as being too hot . . . often a certain bitterness arises, because like the Fisher King of the legend they can neither live with the new consciousness nor can they entirely drop it.'[1]

In St John of the Cross the 'holy wound', though painful in the extreme, is welcomed as a blessing, because the One who wounds is also the One who heals:

> O happy wound, wrought by one who knows how to heal!
> O fortunate and choicest wound; you were made only
>   for delight,
> And the quality of your affliction is gratification for the
>   wounded soul!
> You are great, O delightful wound, because he who caused
>   you is great!

And your delight is great because the fire of love is
infinite and makes you delightful according to your
capacity and greatness.[2]

CRCRCRCRCRCR ☼ ೞೞೞೞೞೞ

ೞ *18* ೞ

The lover's embrace

> 2.6   O that his left hand were under my head,
>   and that his right hand embraced me!

Ellen Davis writes: 'The NRSV translation implies that this is an
unfulfilled wish, but the Hebrew can be more readily understood
as a statement of accomplished fact. The couple are embracing,
and therefore she is "weak/faint/sick" with love.'[1] The woman feels
herself to be supported, held and embraced by her lover's physical
touch.

Commentators have remarked on the parallels here with ancient
Mesopotamian fertility cults, especially the sacred marriage of gods
of fertility. Yet, as both Davis and Edmée Kingsmill point out, there
are marked differences in tone and substance between these pagan
hymns and the Song. 'If the marriage in the Song is ever physically
consummated, we are told that only indirectly in 5.1.'[2] Fertility is not
mentioned, nor children, whereas elsewhere in the Scriptures offspring
are the most important outcome of human love. Love in the Song
has no purpose outside itself. It is the delight in intimacy that is its
only purpose.

God is a passionate lover who will settle for nothing other than
Israel's reciprocal love, nor anything less than ours. From Origen
onwards the verse has been interpreted as an expression of Christ's
passionate love for the human soul, wrapping the soul in prayer,
and also of the pain caused to it in this state by prayer being
interrupted.

CRCRCRCRCRCR ☼ ೞೞೞೞೞೞ

☙ 19 ❧

The heart's time

> 2.7   I adjure you, O daughters of Jerusalem,
>   by the gazelles or the wild does:
>   do not stir up or awaken love
>   until it is ready!

This verse is doubly mysterious. Why does the woman (or is it the poet?) address the daughters of Jerusalem so solemnly, urging them to make an oath? And why make an oath by the names of wild animals? This type of oath is found nowhere else in the Bible, although, interestingly, a similar oath occurs in the Qur'an.[1]

In many cultures, from Greek and Hebrew to Japanese, wild deer are seen as bridging the earthly and spiritual realms, embodying and leading us into the symbolic, intermediate realm of the soul. The Venerable Bede described gazelles and wild does as clean and pure, and therefore as symbolizing spiritual virtues.

These animals could represent wisdom – that is, God's Wisdom.[2] In the Christian legend of St Eustace, a stag enters a dark forest in order to draw the soldier hunting it away from his colleagues so that the stag can 'hunt the hunter while he hunts, finally confronting him with a crucifix miraculously sprouting between its shoulders'.[3] Thus 'the hunter and the hunted are secretly identical'; 'the seeker and the spiritual goal, as well as the pathway to it, are one and the same.'[4]

In some cultures wild deer are believed to symbolize freedom, beauty and strength. There may also be a word play here with certain divine titles, such as the Lord of Hosts (*Adonai Tsva'ot*) and God Almighty (*El Shaddai*) where the consonants in the words for gazelles and wild does are identical or very similar.[5] So it may be that the poet is consciously linking the ideas of freedom, beauty and strength not only with the lover and his beloved, but also indirectly with God.[6]

The second puzzle is this. Why is the beloved woman (or the poet) so concerned that love should not be stirred up or awakened? The very same urgent demand to swear an oath occurs again in the next chapter in a repeated verse.[7] The clue is perhaps at the beginning of this section, where the beloved has declared that her lover has brought her into 'the house of wine': symbolically, into a state of contemplative prayer. This state has brought about a sleep of the ordinary senses, which is not to be disturbed or broken by those who are not within such a state.

The best comment on this verse is to be found in the homilies of St Gregory of Nyssa.

> This sleep is quite extraordinary and different from one's natural habit, for in natural sleep one is not awake. Both are opposed to each other, for sleep and waking succeed and follow each other. We see in the bride a new, paradoxical mixture of the opposites. 'I sleep', she says, 'but my heart is awake.' What can we understand by this statement? This sleep is like death. In it each sensory function of the body is lost; there is no vision, hearing, scent, taste, nor feeling, but the body's tension is loosed . . . Once all these senses have been put to sleep and are gripped by inaction, the heart's action is pure; reason looks above while it remains undisturbed and free from the senses' movement.[8]

St Gregory writes about a spiritual experience that is not at all uncommon among those who practise contemplative prayer – a time, albeit quite brief, maybe just a few moments, in which all the external senses are lulled and the praying person is able to focus attention entirely on God, without self-consciousness.

This same experience is spoken of by the author of *The Cloud of Unknowing*:

> And so attend to this work of contemplation and the marvellous way it operates within your soul. For, truly understood, it is just a sudden and as it were unforeseen stirring, springing swiftly to God like a spark from a coal. And it is marvellous how many stirrings can occur in an hour that is given to this work. And yet, in just one of these stirrings, it can happen that *you forget the whole created world, suddenly and completely.* But straight after each stirring, because of the flesh's corruption, the soul falls back down into some thought or action, done or not done. But what of that? For straight afterwards it rises again as suddenly as it did before.[9]

The essence of contemplative prayer is undivided attention to God: in other words, pure prayer, prayer unmixed with any thoughts, ideas, images, plans, conscious desires for material blessings or even spiritual benefits. It is the prayer not of words or of the intellect, but rather the silent prayer of the heart, by which 'with a devout and delightful stirring of love, [you] struggle to pierce that darkness above you; and beat on that thick cloud of unknowing with a sharp dart of longing love'.[10]

CR CR CR CR CR CR ✿ ꕥ ꕥ ꕥ ꕥ ꕥ ꕥ

CR *20* CR

He is the Rose of Sharon

Here is rather a different take on the images of this second chapter of the Song. Ann Griffiths,[1] as noted above, was a young woman deeply affected by the Methodist Revival, and by her Bible reading. For her it is not the bride but the bridegroom Jesus whom she recognizes as the Rose of Sharon. Identifying herself with the passionate woman of the Song, she sees Jesus as the one who is stunningly attractive ('My beloved is all radiant and ruddy, distinguished among ten thousand'[2]) yet holding himself out of reach in the shadows of the dark trees.

> **I saw him standing**
> Under the dark trees, there he stands,
> there he stands; shall he not draw my eyes?
> I thought I knew a little
> how he compels, beyond all things, but now
> he stands there in the shadows. It will be
> Oh, such a daybreak, such bright morning,
> when I shall wake to see him
> as he is.
>
> He is called Rose of Sharon, for his skin
> is clear, his skin is flushed with blood,
> his body lovely and exact; how he compels
> beyond ten thousand rivals. There he stands
> my friend, the friend of guilt and helplessness,
> to steer my hollow body
> over the sea.

The earth is full of masks and fetishes,
what is there here for me? Are these like him?
Keep company with him and you will know:
no kin, no likeness to those empty eyes.
He is a stranger to them all, great Jesus.
What is there here for me? I know
what I have longed for. Him to hold
me always.

Ann Griffiths (1776–1805)[3]

ෆෆෆෆෆෆෆ ✿ ෩෩෩෩෩෩

ෆ*21*ෆ

Love is swift of foot

2.8   The voice of my beloved!
       Look, he comes,
    leaping upon the mountains,
       bounding over the hills.
2.9   My beloved is like a gazelle
       or a young stag.
    Look, there he stands
       behind our wall,
    gazing in at the windows,
       looking through the lattice.
2.10   My beloved speaks and says to me:
    'Arise, my love, my fair one,
       and come away;'

'The voice of my beloved.' In the book of Jeremiah the prophet speaks in three successive passages of scenes of desolation, of times when God had caused to cease 'the voice of joy, and the voice of gladness, the voice of the bridegroom, and the voice of the bride'. Then comes the great reversal, a God-given restoration: 'Again there shall be heard in this place . . . the voice of joy, and the voice of gladness, the voice of the bridegroom and the voice of the bride'.[1] So 'the voice of my beloved' symbolizes God, who is now restoring Jerusalem, the city standing for all the people of God, brought into perfect communion with their God. In the language of Wisdom, the beloved presents her lover as like a gazelle or a young hart, leaping over the mountains, bounding over the hills, and coming to arouse her and take her to a place of bliss, and we have already discovered the rich symbolic significance of wild deer in the commentary on Song 2.7 above.

In these verses we also hear the repeated invitation: 'My beloved speaks and says to me: "Arise, my love, my fair one, and come away".'[2] The language is striking and has echoes elsewhere: 'Arise, shine; for your light has come,' proclaims the prophet of Babylon as he foretells the ingathering of those who have been scattered in exile – a time of national restoration, and spiritual renewal.[3] God's call to his people may take the form of an invitation to seek his face, or to receive his free gifts. So in the Psalms we find: '"Come," my heart says, "seek his face!" Your face, LORD, do I seek.'[4] And again in Isaiah, to all those who are spiritually thirsty:

> Come to the waters . . . come, buy wine and milk without money and without price . . . Incline your ear, and come to me; listen so that you may live. I will make with you an everlasting covenant, my steadfast, sure love for David.[5]

God's promises are renewed, and will be finally fulfilled in the coming of the son of David, in the Word made flesh in Jesus.

> Love comes leaping over the mountains of our resistance, bounding over the hills of our refusal. Love sings: 'Come away. Come with me. Let me bring you with me into God.' The heart, still frozen by the winter of its hardening, sleeps.
>
> But now he is here, standing behind the wall, peering through the lattice. But he never, ever, forces his way in.[6]

CRCRCRCRCRCR ☼ ßÜßÜßÜßÜßÜßÜ

෬22෬

Winter is past

2.11 'for now the winter is past,
the rain is over and gone.

2.12   The flowers appear on the earth;
the time of singing has come,
and the voice of the turtle-dove
is heard in our land.

2.13   The fig tree puts forth its figs,
and the vines are in blossom;
they give forth fragrance.
Arise, my love, my fair one,
and come away.'

These verses form one of the best-known passages in the Song. They are a favourite choice at weddings, and in some lectionaries are selected as a canticle or reading for a summer Sunday.

'for now the winter is past,
the rain is over and gone . . .'

Once again, with eyes and nose and ear, the reader is, as it were, invited to feast on the sights, scents and sounds of spring after the long months of bitter cold. It is a glimpse of heaven, either of the earthly variety or of heaven above. The profusion of flowers following winter is part of nature's cycle, and denotes a season that proverbially brings out lovers. But for our poet, as for other writers, the end of winter and the spring flowers have a metaphorical meaning. Shakespeare famously put these words into the mouth of King Richard III at the beginning of the play of that name: 'Now is the winter of our discontent made glorious by this sun of York.'

As we have already seen, flowers are associated not only with the spring, but with national restoration and renewal.[1] They appear as symbols of the restored beauty of Israel and Jerusalem, after a time of alienation from God and devastation by her enemies. Isaiah says that 'the wilderness shall blossom like the rose'.[2] Hosea predicts that 'Israel . . . shall blossom like the vine, and his remembrance [or his fragrance] shall be like the wine of Lebanon'.[3] So it is that even while Jerusalem was under attack from her enemies, instead of despairing, Jeremiah buys land in his own village in the confidence that under God his people will one day return from exile in Babylon to their beloved homeland.[4]

This sense of a profusion of flowers, beautiful and fragrant, is a powerful image. For the prophets, the blooming of Israel's semi-desert landscape is a metaphor of the people being restored to a faithful covenant relationship. It seems likely that the poet of the Song has in mind also a restoration, an imaginative return to the Garden of Eden, to Paradise, in God's time. For now 'the winter is past', the centuries of alienation when the love between Israel and God had grown cold, is over.

In C. S. Lewis' *The Lion, the Witch and the Wardrobe*, the land of Narnia and all its animals and plants are held in the grip of deep winter by the power of the evil White Witch. The four children who have arrived there from earth can liberate the land from the deep winter only by allying themselves with the lion Aslan. Aslan, the King of Beasts, son of the Emperor-Over-the-Sea, is a wise, compassionate, magical authority (both temporal and spiritual), a mysterious and benevolent guide to the visiting children, the guardian and saviour of Narnia. Lewis once described Aslan as the form in which Christ might have appeared in a fantasy world. So in order for the land to be saved Aslan must offer himself to be sacrificed. Salvation comes only with the noble self-sacrifice of the greatest and strongest of all the beasts, the King of the animal kingdom.[5]

Just as the symbolism of spring can be a sign of a national restoration, or the revival of faith, hope and love among the faithful, this metaphor also works at the level of the individual, whether it is an artist, a poet, or a soul longing for spiritual renewal.

George Herbert's poem 'The Flower' expresses the poet's sense of a renewal of his 'shrivel'd heart' recovering its 'greenness' after a spiritual winter of 'hard weather'. He sees his recovery as entirely the work of God. Just as nature continues to do its work unseen, so grace operates invisibly in the human soul. Times of seeming deadness, an experience of desolation, are often those when God does his greatest work within our souls. It is only afterwards that we see and marvel at what has been happening: 'These are thy wonders, Lord of love, to make us see we are but flowers that glide.'

The Flower

How fresh, O Lord, how sweet and clean
Are thy returns! ev'n as the flowers in spring;
  To which, besides their own demean,[6]
The late-past frosts tributes of pleasure bring.
  Grief melts away

Like snow in May,
As if there were no such cold thing.

Who would have thought my shrivel'd heart
Could have recover'd greenness? It was gone
Quite under ground; as flowers depart
To see their mother-root, when they have blown;
Where they together
All the hard weather,
Dead to the world, keep house unknown.

These are thy wonders, Lord of power,
Killing and quick'ning,[7] bringing down to hell
And up to heaven in an hour;
Making a chiming of a passing-bell,
We say amiss,
This or that is:
Thy word is all, if we could spell.

These are thy wonders, Lord of love,
To make us see we are but flowers that glide:[8]
Which when we once can find and prove,[9]
Thou hast a garden for us, where to bide.
Who would be more,
Swelling through store,
Forfeit their Paradise by their pride.

ෲෲෲෲෲෲ ✿ ෴෴෴෴෴෴

ෲ23ෲ

Longing

2.14 'O my dove, in the clefts of the rock,
in the covert of the cliff.
let me see your face,
let me hear your voice;
for your voice is sweet,
and your face is lovely.'

For as long as the story of Noah's ark has been told, the dove bearing the olive leaf has been associated with *shalom* – peace – and here she symbolizes Israel at peace. The dove inhabits a hidden place of security given her by God, who has chosen her to be his people. In some Hebrew traditions Paradise is pictured as a mountain.

The fascinating point for us here is that the divine Lover, just like any male suitor, is beseeching his beloved that he may see her face and hear her sweet voice. The beloved is, of course, free to respond as she wishes, affirmatively or negatively. God leads, chooses, disciplines, empowers, heals, loves, demands, pleads, but never forces his will on his people, or on any individual. He does not attempt to control his beloved. Thus Christ addresses the lukewarm church of Laodicea:

> I reprove and discipline those whom I love. Be earnest, therefore, and repent. Listen, I am standing at the door, knocking; if you hear my voice and open the door, I will come in to you and eat with you, and you with me.[1]

At Christ's baptism the descent of the Holy Spirit is symbolized by a dove.[2] Where does this image come from? One early Jewish source associates the phrase 'the voice of the turtle-dove' with the Spirit.[3] In Genesis we read that 'a wind [or spirit] of God swept over the face of the (primeval) waters'. An early Jewish gloss on this verse added the words 'like a dove'.[4] So the image of the dove came from Jewish tradition into the Gospels and was adopted as a regular feature of Christian iconography. Christ's baptism was seen as marking a new beginning, a new creation, the age of the Spirit: an event that prepared his followers for the outpouring of the Spirit on the whole Church at Pentecost.

> O King enthroned on high,
> thou Comforter divine,
> blest Spirit of all truth, be nigh
> and make us thine.
>
> Thou art the source of life,
> thou art our treasure-store;
> Give us thy peace, and end our strife
> for evermore.

Descend, O heavenly Dove,
abide with us always;
and in the fullness of thy love
cleanse us, we pray.

Greek, *c.* eighth century[5]

෪෪෪෪෪෪෪ ☼ ෫෫෫෫෫෫

෪24෫

Threats

2.15 'Catch us the foxes,
the little foxes,
that ruin the vineyards –
for our vineyards are in blossom.'

Although the poet is presenting us with a picture of Paradise, this verse suggests that there are still dangers to watch out for. Since ancient times, foxes were known as creatures that plundered the vineyards. Foxes may not be dangerous compared with lions or bears, yet in the Venerable Bede's phrase, 'they are exceedingly devious animals, that hide themselves in ditches or caves and when they come out they *never run along straight paths but in twisting circles*'.[1] Bede suggests that they are like the deceptions and deceits of heretics: people who choose what they want to believe rather than accept the faith handed down within Holy Scripture and the Church's rule of faith. They should not be destroyed but be 'caught', so that they may be put right.

In today's spiritual climate, the use of the word 'heretic' may arouse suspicions of bigotry or dogmatism, especially if it is heard as a term of abuse or authoritarian power. But if the Church is to retain its soul and be a beacon for the truth of the good news of the gospel, it must be vigilant against those who would water down, distort or weaken its essential message.

John Henry Newman's hymn is a robust poem of faith in the three central doctrines of the Christian faith: God the Holy Trinity, the saving work and Passion of Christ, true Man and true God, and the power of God's grace in our human lives.

Firmly I believe and truly
God is Three and God is One;
And I next acknowledge duly
Manhood taken by the Son.

And I trust and hope most fully
in that manhood crucified;
And each thought and deed unruly
do to death, as he has died.

Simply to his grace and wholly
light and life and strength belong,
And I love supremely, solely,
him the holy, him the strong

And I hold in veneration,
for the love of him alone,
Holy Church as his creation,
and her teachings as his own.

                              J. H. Newman (1801–90)[2]

         ೞೞೞೞೞೞ ☼ ೞೞೞೞೞೞ

ೞ *25* ೞ

Fleeting beauty

2.16   My beloved is mine and I am his;
          he pastures his flock among the lilies.
2.17   Until the day breathes
          and the shadows flee,
       turn, my beloved, be like a gazelle
          or a young stag on the cleft of the mountains.

(For 2.16 see the commentary on 6.3.)

'Until the day breathes and the shadows flee' are words that are
repeated in 4.6, where the poet continues: 'I will hasten to the mountain
of myrrh and the hill of frankincense.' The mountain of myrrh and
the hill of frankincense, as we will see, both point to the Temple and

Mount Zion.[1] The time when the day breathes and the shadows flee is daybreak, when thank-offerings would be made. Here in verse 17, as in verse 9, the woman once again sees her beloved as a gazelle or a young stag, full of life and beauty, but at the same time fleeting and elusive. We will meet this same image in the last verse of the Song. The divine Lover's presence can never be guaranteed or demanded, but the woman is again taking the initiative in her bidding to him.

Jan Struther, the pen name of Joyce Anstruther, achieved fame in the late 1930s when she created the character of Mrs Miniver. Although claiming to be an agnostic, she wrote some hymns for children, of which 'Lord of all hopefulness' is one of the most well known and best loved. Its call on the Lord to be present, with his gifts of love and grace, from daybreak to the end of the day seems to fit this verse in the Song.

> Lord of all hopefulness, Lord of all joy,
> whose trust, ever childlike, no care could destroy,
> be there at our waking, and give us, we pray,
> your bliss in our hearts, Lord,
> at the break of the day.
>
> Lord of all kindliness, Lord of all grace,
> your hands swift to welcome, your arms to embrace,
> be there at our homing, and give us, we pray,
> your love in our hearts, Lord,
> at the eve of the day.
>
> Jan Struther (1901–53)[2]

ෆෆෆෆෆෆ ✿ ෩෩෩෩෩෩

ෆ 26 ෆ

Seeking and not finding

3.1 Upon my bed at night
I sought him whom my soul loves.
I sought him, but found him not;
I called him but he gave no answer.

3.2 'I will rise now and go about the city,
    in the streets and in the squares;
    I will seek whom my soul loves.'
    I sought him, but found him not.

3.3 The sentinels found me,
    as they went about in the city.
    'Have you seen him whom my soul loves?'

Lovers may well know the experience of a profound longing, when even an ordinary absence of the beloved can seem hardly bearable. The longing is often felt most acutely at night. The woman's yearning turns to anxiety, as she twice says: 'I sought him, but found him not.' At first she voices her anxiety privately to herself, but then goes out of the house to the public streets, where she asks the city watchmen: 'Have you seen him whom my soul loves?'

The most striking feature of her speech, both to herself and to the city watchmen, is the way she describes her lover as 'him whom my soul loves' not once but four times. This cannot be a slip of the tongue or pen. It must be a deliberate expression. Could it be an allusion to the *shema*, the great commandment of the Jewish Torah designated by Jesus as the first commandment? 'You shall love the LORD your God with all your heart, and with all your soul, and with all your might.'[1] If this is so, then the one who is sought here so intensely is no human lover, but none other than God himself.

In Moses' final address to the Israelites on the threshold of the Promised Land, he foresees their disobedience and exile from their homeland. But he also assures them that they will return. He says to them: 'From [a foreign land] you will seek the LORD your God, and you will find him if you search after him with all your heart and soul.'[2] This theme of searching for God with serious intent is one that is repeated in the prophets: 'When you search for me, you will find me; if you seek me with all your heart.'[3]

Tragically, Israel often refused to look for God, and turned to those whom Hosea so often calls 'her lovers' – that is, foreign idols.

But such turning away from God, her only true and faithful lover, leads the people down a blind alley, to futility and frustration. So, for example, in the last chapters of Isaiah, dating from the time of the Exile, we hear of God's anguish in these poignant words:

I was ready to be sought out by those who did not ask,
  to be found by those who did not seek me.
I said, 'Here I am, here I am',
  to a nation that did not call on my name.[4]

It is a common experience in human relationships that when one partner seems to have backed away or cooled off, the very fear felt by the other
partner of losing the beloved may itself purify the desire, and make the
relationship more durable and stable. One of the lessons to be learned
from the experience of St John of the Cross is that God's elusiveness
may serve to strengthen truly spiritual love, a love that rises above our
immediate material needs. Often wisdom and maturity are attained
when we wake up to the discovery that we cannot live without this love.

The initial phrase, 'Upon my bed at night I sought him', points to
a non-literal interpretation for this theme of seeking and finding.
Certainly, no unmarried Israelite woman living with her mother could
realistically expect to find her lover in her bed! In the Scriptures the
bed is a place not only for sleeping and making love, but for reflection, for the prayer of silence, and even for singing! In the Psalms,
for example, we are told: 'When you are disturbed, do not be angry;
ponder it on your beds, and be silent'; and 'Let the faithful exult in
glory; let them sing for joy on their couches.'[5]

The frustration felt in seeking God and not finding him is common
to both mystics and saints, as it is for all who attempt the prayer of
stillness and silence. St Teresa of Avila found herself complaining to
God: 'how is it that when there is so little time left over to enjoy Your
presence You hide from me?' She asks, 'How is this compatible with
Your mercy? How can the love You bear me allow this? . . . I implore
You to see that it is injurious to one who loves You so much!'[6]

CBCBCBCBCBCB ☼ BOBOBOBOBOBO

CB*27*CB

Seeking and now finding

3.4 Scarcely had I passed them,
      when I found him whom my soul loves.

> I held him, and would not let him go
> until I brought him into my mother's house,
> and into the chamber of her that conceived me.
3.5 I adjure you, O daughters of Jerusalem,
> by the gazelles or the wild does:
> do not stir up or awaken love
> until it is ready!

The woman's anxiety comes to an abrupt end. All of a sudden she finds her lover, grabs him, and pulls him through the streets to her mother's home! An extraordinary scenario, almost comic, and one that certainly must appear quite contrary to the prevailing patriarchal culture. An unmarried woman was expected to stay at home in her father's house until a suitable mate was found for her by her parents, or perhaps by her older brothers. Her brothers are referred to in the first chapter of the Song, and again at the end, as people who treat her badly, making her work for them in their vineyards, and then trying to control her.[1] Yet her mother is mentioned seven times, and seven is the number that represents completeness, just as there are seven days in the week. Apart from the book of Ruth, the Song is the only book in the Bible that looks at the world through the eyes of women.

Later in the Song, the woman speaks not of her desire for her lover, as she does here and in the first chapter, but of her lover's desire for her.[2] We will return to this point later. So what do we make of these lines in the Song, where the woman is said to bring back her lover to 'my mother's house, and into the chamber of her that conceived me'? This determined young woman seems to be subverting the normal code of behaviour, to be acting in a way that would have brought scandal and disgrace upon her and upon her mother.

These lines give us a vivid picture, but for the reasons given they are hardly to be taken literally. We need to look more deeply. The theme of mother and daughter is a rich one, and points to a common symbol in Holy Scripture. In both the Old Testament and the New, Jerusalem is likened to a mother, because of her character as having the God-given role of nurturing her children. Yet Jerusalem has often failed in that maternal role. The prophet Hosea denounces Israel's betrayal of her vocation: 'For their mother has played the whore, she who conceived them has acted shamefully.'[3]

Famously, in one of his laments over Jerusalem, Jesus saw himself as willing to have undertaken that kind of nurturing maternal role: 'Jerusalem, Jerusalem, the city that kills the prophets and stones those who are sent to it! How often have I desired to gather your children together as a hen gathers her brood under her wings, and you were not willing!' It is of particular interest to us that in Luke's parallel account, Jesus ascribes the words of accusation against the city to the Wisdom of God, which is the only example in the New Testament of God's Wisdom being personified in the same way as it is in the Hebrew Wisdom books.[4]

But here in the Song there is a message of consolation. The lover is coming into the mother's house, and right into the mother's own private room, where the beloved was conceived. This seems to be another allusion to the Temple, the spiritual home of Mother Israel, and to the place of greatest privacy and holiness, the very Holy of Holies. Later in the Song, especially in chapter 4, there are indeed many phrases that suggest that the Temple is being alluded to.

A poem entitled 'In a Country Church' by the Welsh priest-poet R. S. Thomas (1913–2000) beautifully and concisely expresses the spiritual highs and lows of the spiritual life: of perseverance through dry times when prayer appears to be unanswered, and then that moment when comes an unexpected moment of insight or revelation. The poet links Christ's crown of thorns with the image of Moses' burning bush. This poem may also remind us of the story of the conversion of the seventeenth-century young Carmelite Brother Laurence, who had a vision of a tree in wintertime covered with a summer crown of foliage, and was brought to a deep awareness of God's love and care for all his creation.

ෆ ෆ ෆ ෆ ෆ ෆ ☼ ෨ ෨ ෨ ෨ ෨ ෨

ෆ 28 ෆ

Wisdom and true worship

3.6   What is that coming up from the wilderness,
      like a column of smoke,
   perfumed with myrrh and frankincense,
      with all the fragrant powders of the merchant?

3.7   Look, it is the litter of Solomon!
       Around it are sixty mighty men
       of the mighty men of Israel,
3.8   all equipped with swords
       and expert in war:
       each with his sword at his thigh
       because of alarms by night.

At first reading these verses seem to be describing a powerful invasion by a military force. But the NRSV translation here is probably not quite correct. Verse 6 should read not 'What is that . . .' but 'Who is this coming up from the desert . . . ?' Moreover, the word 'this' is a feminine pronoun. It is a person that is being referred to, not a thing.[1] Verse 6 seems to stand on its own, and is another example of how the dream-like character of the Song suddenly leads the reader to an entirely new image. Here the scenario is neither the city, nor fertile countryside, nor forest, but the desert wilderness. There is no reply to the question, 'Who is this coming up from the desert . . . ?', but the likely answer is God's bride: that is, Israel. Thus Jeremiah refers to the Lord's words: 'I remember the devotion of your youth, your love as a bride, how you followed me in the wilderness, in a land not sown.'[2]

In the Song the bride Israel is 'perfumed with myrrh and frankincense', but here is another point. Frankincense is never used as a cosmetic, but only in worship to accompany sacrificial offerings. The bride Israel who comes up to the Temple from the Judean desert is approaching as a pilgrim to make her collective offering to the Lord.

So too the New Israel, the Bride of Christ, we the Church, comes to make her one and only perfect offering at every Eucharist:

Wherefore, O Father, we thy humble servants
here bring before thee Christ thy well-beloved.
all perfect offering, sacrifice immortal,
spotless oblation.

See now, thy children, making intercession
through him our Saviour, Son of God incarnate,
for all thy people, living and departed,
pleading before thee.

William Jervois (1852–1905)[3]

ଔଔଔଔଔଔ ✿ ଌଌଌଌଌଌ

∽29∾

Israel's self-offering and ours

3.7 Look, it is the litter of Solomon!
Around it are sixty mighty men
of the mighty men of Israel,

3.8 all equipped with swords
and expert in war:
each with his sword at his thigh,
because of alarms by night.

3.9 King Solomon made himself a palanquin
from the wood of Lebanon.

3.10 He made its posts of silver,
its back of gold, its seat of purple;
its interior was inlaid with love.
Daughters of Jerusalem,
come out.

3.11 Look, O daughters of Zion,
at King Solomon,
at the crown with which his mother crowned him
on the day of his wedding,
on the day of the gladness of his heart.

In one Jewish rabbinical tradition[1] it is stated that all occurrences of the name 'Solomon' in the Song are sacred (except one, presumably here in verse 11) – that is to say, cryptic references to God. In that case, it is God himself who must be understood to be the true architect and builder of the Temple. The 'palanquin', or light litter, is then a metaphorical reference to the Temple. The 'wood of Lebanon' are the cedars and cypresses sent by King Hiram of Tyre for the Temple, while the silver refers to the 'holy things of his [Solomon's] father David, the silver, the gold and the vessels'.[2] Reference to gold can also be found in the parallel account of the building of the Temple in the first book of Chronicles.[3] The 'interior' which was 'inlaid with love' (or possibly 'mosaic') is the floor of the Temple.

How is it that it is Solomon's mother who crowns him king? St Gregory of Nyssa interprets the meaning by explaining that the terms 'mother' and 'father' mean the same where God is concerned since there is neither male nor female in God. David's wife Bathsheba, mother of Solomon, symbolizes God not on her own account but simply because Solomon was chosen by God to be the symbol of wisdom and peace! St Gregory of Nyssa quotes Psalm 21:

> In your strength the king rejoices, O LORD,
>   and in your help how greatly he exults!
> You have given him his heart's desire,
>   and have not withheld the request of his lips.
> For you meet him with rich blessings;
>   you set a crown of fine gold on his head.
> He asked you for life; you gave it to him –
>   length of days for ever and ever.[4]

An alternative suggestion[5] is that 'mother' here could refer to divine Wisdom, for it was the wisdom desired most by the king in his prayer to God. The female figure of verse 6 could be divine Wisdom, created by God to dwell with Israel. In the book of Sirach, Wisdom, 'who came forth from the mouth of the Most High', is commanded by God to dwell in Zion, the place of the Temple, where 'God gave her a resting place, taking root in an honoured people . . . in the Lord's heritage.'

> O what their joy and their glory must be,
> Those endless Sabbaths the blessed ones see!
> Crown for the valiant; to weary ones rest;
> God shall be all, and in all ever blest.

> Truly Jerusalem name we that shore,
> 'Vision of Peace', that brings joy evermore!
> Wish and fulfilment can severed be ne'er,
> Nor the things prayed for come short of the prayer.[6]
>
> Peter Abelard (1079–1142)

03 03 03 03 03 03 ☼ 80 80 80 80 80 80

03 *30* 03

Beauty and strength

> 4.1 How beautiful you are, my love,
>   how very beautiful!

Your eyes are doves
   behind your veil.
Your hair is like a flock of goats,
   moving down the slopes of Gilead.

4.2 Your teeth are like a flock of shorn ewes
     that have come up from the washing,
  all of which bear twins,
     and not one among them is bereaved.

4.3 Your lips are like a crimson thread,
     and your mouth is lovely.
  Your cheeks are like halves of a pomegranate
     behind your veil.

4.4 Your neck is like the tower of David,
     built in courses;
  on it hang a thousand bucklers,
     all of them shields of warriors.

4.5 Your two breasts are like two fawns,
     twins of a gazelle,
     that feed among the lilies.

4.6 Until the day breathes
     and the shadows flee,
  I will hasten to the mountain of myrrh
     and the hill of frankincense.

4.7 You are altogether beautiful, my love;
     there is no flaw in you.

In what is his first address to her, the male lover admires the beloved in beautiful but extravagant terms.[1] His language is flamboyant and perhaps sounds bizarre to Western ears, and his description may well seem strange in another respect. Having heard or read his words, we still have no idea of what she actually looks like. But this is not unusual for love poetry, and it is one significant factor that distinguishes it from an 'objective description'. The woman's body is not seen in isolation from her natural, geographical and historical context, and that context is important.

The poem refers to seven aspects of her appearance, moving gradually downwards from her eyes to her breasts. The number seven is carefully chosen. It symbolizes completeness, and is summed up in verse 7: 'You are altogether beautiful, my love; there is no flaw in you.'

The similes at first seem quite startling, even ridiculous, but if we recognize that there is just one point of similarity, or at most two, the poetic images work well. A good set of teeth resembles a flock of sheep in its whiteness and relative uniformity of appearance. The beloved's hair is like a flock of goats moving down the hillside, because it is falling or tumbling down her shoulders in black waves or curls. The images of her breasts like 'fawns' suggests softness and beauty, while her neck being like the tower of David suggests strength. And the reference to David also suggests that this strength is given by God.

The two lovers are pictured in the context of a paradise, a Garden of Eden restored, bursting with natural and human life; the lovers share it with sheep and goats, gazelles and foxes, lions and leopards, abundant fruit, flowers, spices, scented timber, silver, gold and bronze. The effect is glorious: a glimpse of heaven on earth.

Read metaphorically, the beloved once again symbolizes the Temple and particularly the Holy of Holies, and thus the language is perfectly apt. The reference to goats' hair, for example, as in the first chapter of the Song,[2] could well allude to the curtains of the Holy of Holies.

Gilead brings to mind a series of stories connected with the foundational period of Israel's history. The name Gilead occurs three times in the story of the conflict between Laban and his nephew Jacob. It is where the two eventually make peace, and where Jacob sets up a pillar on which he makes sacrifice.[3] In this story, too, are references to ewes, and to female goats which did not miscarry. Jacob is always significant because he was renamed by God as Israel, and so comes to personify the nation.[4] The remembrance of that early history is important for Israel, and so for the poet of the Song. Throughout that history God is seen as always in command of events, and ever revealing his loving kindness.

It is this loving relationship between God and Israel (and for us, the Church, the new Israel) that most interests us. In this connection Kingsmill cites a text from an early Jewish mystical tradition in which a quasi-marital relationship between God and his people Israel is clearly implied:

And bear witness to them of what you see of me; what I do to the countenance of Jacob, your father, which is engraved by me

87

on the throne of my Glory. For at the time when you recite before me Holy! Holy! Holy! . . . I bend down towards him and caress him, embrace him and kiss him, with my hands upon his arms three times, corresponding to the three times at which you recite . . . the Holy, Holy, Holy is the Lord of Hosts.[5]

$$\text{ } \text{ } \text{ } \text{ } \text{ } \text{ } \text{ } \text{ } ☼ \text{ } \text{ } \text{ } \text{ } \text{ } \text{ }$$

♋ 31 ♋

Duality in nature

> 4.2　Your teeth are like a flock of shorn ewes
> that have come up from the washing.

According to the Targum,[1] the teeth of the beloved are a metaphor for the two matching orders of priests and Levites who eat the priestly gifts; it also identifies the flock as Jacob's flock. Jacob possesses ewes, and he also loves Rachel, whose name means 'ewe'. Jacob and Esau are twins, and throughout the first five verses of chapter 4 there is a noticeable concentration on doubles or pairs – two sets of teeth, the bearing of twins, a pair of lips, two breasts like two fawns. It seems that the poet is drawing on a tradition found in Sirach, one of the books of Wisdom, that 'all things are twofold, one opposite the other', a symbol perhaps of complementarity, to be expected or hoped for in lovers, and certainly implicit in the Genesis story of the creation of Eve from the side of Adam.[2] Here also the two breasts are symbols of the two tablets of the Law, just as fawns or harts are symbols of Wisdom.

The description of the beloved's neck being like 'David's tower' is puzzling, but may perhaps be a cryptic reference to the Temple, which was sometimes called a tower. Although it was David's son who built the Temple, the idea and the design came from David. The phrase 'built in courses' sounds like rows of ornaments on the beloved's neck, and so may suggest the rising terraces of an imposing sacred building constructed like a Babylonian ziggurat. Shields were used to decorate walls, including the walls of the Temple.[3]

Finally, the Lover declares: 'You are altogether beautiful, my love; there is no flaw in you.' There is a significant link between this verse and a passage about marriage and the Church in the letter to Ephesians, where the author, consciously or unconsciously, draws on the language of the Song:

> Husbands love your wives, as Christ loved the Church, and gave himself up for her, that he might sanctify her, having cleansed her by the washing of water with the word, that he might present the Church to himself in splendour, without spot or wrinkle or any such thing, that she might be holy and *without blemish*.[4]

Here the word for 'without blemish' is exactly the same in the Greek Septuagint version of the Song. Both the poet and the author of the epistle are writing about the same thing: the Temple (and thus the Church), the beloved who is to be the bride.

> The Church's one foundation
> is Jesus Christ her Lord;
> she is his new creation
> by water and the word:
> from heaven he came and sought her
> to be his holy Bride
> with his own blood he bought her,
> and for her life he died.
> Samuel John Stone (1839–1900)[5]

ෆෆෆෆෆෆ ✿ ෨෨෨෨෨෨

ෆ*32*ෆ

The Song of Lebanon

4.8 Come with me from Lebanon, my bride;
    come with me from Lebanon.
Depart from the peak of Amana,
    from the peak of Senir and Hermon,
from the dens of lions,
    from the mountains of leopards.

4.9   You have ravished my heart, my sister, my bride,
       you have ravished my heart with a glance of your eyes,
       with one jewel of your necklace.

4.10   How sweet is your love, my sister, my bride!
       how much better is your love than wine,
       and the fragrance of your oils than any spice!

4.11   Your lips distil nectar, my bride;
       honey and milk are under your tongue;
       the scent of your garments is like the scent of Lebanon.

4.12   A garden locked is my sister, my bride,
       a garden locked, a fountain sealed.

4.13   Your channel is an orchard of pomegranates
       with all choicest fruits,
       henna with nard,

4.14   nard and saffron, calamus and cinnamon,
       with all trees of frankincense,
       myrrh and aloes,
       with all chief spices –

4.15   a garden fountain, a well of living water,
       and flowing streams from Lebanon.

Here for the first time the beloved is addressed as 'my bride', and this title is repeated again and again in the following section. For this reason many take this to be a marriage scene, especially as the language rises to a peak of sensual and emotional intensity. But there are also strong hints that the poet is deliberately evoking 'a quality of mystery and wonder, for the language suggests intense religious as well as sexual experience'.[1]

Every line here echoes other biblical texts, especially the Prophets and Psalms, and the description of Solomon's Temple in 1 Kings.[2] There is a depth to this section of the Song that can only be grasped by those who read it in the context of the Hebrew Scriptures as a whole.

The next point of interest is that the image of the garden has now become paramount. It was suggested earlier[3] that the Song as a whole is a celebration of a spring – like a return to Eden following a long winter of alienation from God. Here is imagined a restoration of the original intimacy between God and humanity, in which the Temple is none other than the Garden of Eden. Thus 'the Song aims to draw us into the experience of ultimate intimacy that is the reward of the pilgrim, the devoted lover of God'.[4]

Also notable is the emphasis on Lebanon. In the whole of the Song it is referred to seven times – the number of completeness – and four of these references come in these eight verses, hence its name, 'the Song of Lebanon'. But what is the significance of Lebanon here and in the Song as a whole? For the people of Israel, the first thing that would have come to mind was that Lebanon provided the huge quantity of cedar logs that were used in the construction of the Temple. The mountain peaks of the border country, including Mount Hermon (4.8),[5] were known in ancient times as 'the cedar mountain, abode of the gods, throne-seat of Ishtar'.[6] So it is also suggested that the cedars of Lebanon were valued not just for their beauty and scent, but for their aura of divine mystery, coming as they did from the mythical abode of the gods. So Mount Zion becomes 'a new cedar mountain, a divine abode that supersedes that of the ancient gods',[7] and Lebanon becomes a code word for Jerusalem's glory as God's dwelling place. In the last chapters of Isaiah, dating from after the destruction of Jerusalem and Solomon's Temple, we read: 'The glory of Lebanon shall come to you', meaning that God will restore the Temple to its former glory.[8]

Lebanon features more than once in the Gospel narratives. Its most important association for us is that it was at Caesarea Philippi, beneath Mount Hermon in Lebanon, 'the cosmic mountain which joins earth with lowest heaven', that Jesus challenged his disciples to answer the great existential question of the Gospels: who do you say that I am?[9]

> To be Jesus' disciple means to allow one's own identity to be stamped by the identity of the one who died forsaken on the cross. When we embrace Mark's answer to the question 'Who do you say that I am?' we are not just making a theological affirmation about Jesus' identity; we are choosing our own identity as well.[10]

Jesus said: 'I am the way, the truth, and the life.'[11] This beautiful short poem by George Herbert expresses and develops these three aspects of Jesus' true identity.

The Call
Come my Way, my Truth, my Life:
Such a Way, as gives us breath:

Such a Truth, as ends all strife:
And such a Life, as killeth death.

Come, my Light, my Feast, my Strength:
Such a Light, as shows a feast:
Such a Feast, as mends in length:
Such a Strength, as makes his guest.

Come my Joy, my Love, my Heart:
Such a Joy, as none can move:
Such a Love, as none can part:
Such a Heart, as joys in love.

ෆෆෆෆෆෆ ✿ ꙮꙮꙮꙮꙮꙮ

ෆ*33*ෆ

The ravished heart

4.9   You have ravished my heart, my sister, my bride,
          you have ravished my heart with a glance of your eyes,
       with one jewel of your necklace.
4.10 How sweet is your love, my sister, my bride!
       how much better is your love than wine,
       and the fragrance of your oils than any spice!

The often-repeated phrase 'my sister, my bride' may be puzzling. Sibling marriages were not permitted in Israel.[1] But the phrase is common in Egyptian love poetry, one of the influences behind the Song, and it simply indicates that there is total affinity between the lovers. Situated here, halfway through the poem, the expression may suggest that a deeper relationship has now been reached between the two lovers, a profound sense of oneness, going beyond the physical and the emotional to a union of mind, body and soul.

And that leads us to a more general but important point. Although this is a contemplative guide to the Song, in which our dominant interest is in the less obvious reading, here, as in some other passages,[2] it is impossible to ignore the obvious language of human love. As has been already argued, it is best to read the Song as a poem of multiple meanings or layers.[3] The 'literal' and the 'metaphorical' readings in no way contradict each other, but both enhance the meaning. Divine love may indeed excel all other loves, but it does not diminish them. We may liken the poem to a kaleidoscope where just a tiny movement of the finger changes the pattern.

Looking closely, we see at one moment a human love scene, and a young woman who is both beautiful and chaste ('garden locked' v.12). Then we blink, and now we see the special intimacy between God and Israel, which reaches its high point in Temple worship. Neither finally succeeds the other as the *one* correct interpretation, but the mind continually oscillates between the two.[4]

The second half of this verse repeats almost exactly the opening verses of the Song, but this time it is the man who addresses the woman. The love they have for each other is mutual and equal.

Jacob wrestled with an angel all night at the ford of Jabbok, and would not let him go until he had received a blessing.[5] But there was a cost. Jacob was left with a limp because of injury to his hip. Religious poets use images not only of human love but also of violent combat in order to express the relationship between the soul and God. The word 'ravish' originally meant to seize booty. The phrase 'You have ravished my heart' suggests taking by storm, and by extension an enchantment. In one of his many images for prayer George Herbert writes of 'engine against th'Almighty': that is, a battering ram.[6] The importunate widow in Jesus' parable would not give up bothering the unjust judge until he had given her a hearing.[7]

The same image of 'battering' is used by John Donne in one of his Holy Sonnets, but in reverse, to suggest that only by allowing God to 'batter my heart' and 'bend your force, to break, blow, burn, and make me new', can he be truly liberated from betrothal to God's enemy. He does not believe that he himself has the power to accept the invitation to love God without God's direct action.

Batter my heart, three-person'd God; for you
As yet but knock; breathe, shine, and seek to mend;
That I may rise, and stand, o'erthrow me, and bend
Your force, to break, blow, burn, and make me new.
I, like an usurp'd town, to another due,
Labour to admit you, but O, to no end.
Reason, your viceroy in me, me should defend,

But is captived, and proves weak or untrue.
Yet dearly I love you, and would be loved fain,
But am betroth'd unto your enemy;
Divorce me, untie, or break that knot again,
Take me to you, imprison me, for I,
Except you enthrall me, never shall be free,
Nor ever chaste, except you ravish me.[8]

ೞೞೞೞೞೞೞ ☼ ೞೞೞೞೞೞ

ೞ 34 ೞ

The Garden and the Temple (1)

4.12   A garden locked is my sister, my bride,
       a garden locked, a fountain sealed.

4.13   Your channel is an orchard of pomegranates,
       with all choicest fruits,
   henna with nard,

4.14   nard and saffron, calamus and cinnamon,
       with all trees of frankincense,
   myrrh and aloes
       with all chief spices –

4.15   a garden fountain, a well of living water,
       and flowing streams from Lebanon.

4.16   Awake, O north wind,
       and come, O south wind!
   Blow upon my garden
       that its fragrance may be wafted abroad.
   Let my beloved come to his garden,
       and eat its choicest fruits.

5.1   I come to my garden, my sister, my bride;
       I gather my myrrh with my spice,
   I eat my honeycomb with my honey,
   I drink my wine with my milk.
   Eat, friends, drink,
       and be drunk with love.

Paradise

The archetypal symbol of the Garden of Eden links the Song with the first chapters of the Bible. Apart from in Genesis, nowhere else in the Scriptures are there so many occurrences of the word 'garden'. The Septuagint[1] word for the Garden of Eden, and here in the Song, is *paradeisos*, which derives from a Persian word *pardes*, meaning a walled garden. So Paradise is identified with the Garden of Eden, which was closed (walled up) after the expulsion of Adam and Eve. In Hebrew tradition there was an expectation that one day Paradise would be opened again. 'Paradise, then, became strongly associated with hope for the end times, and with the idea that in those end-times Paradise would be re-opened and the righteous allowed to eat from the tree of life and hence to live for ever.'[2] This certainly seems to be the use of the word 'paradise' in Revelation: 'To everyone who conquers, I will give permission to eat from the tree of life that is in the paradise of God.'[3]

That the end times had already arrived with the death and resurrection of Christ appears also to be implied when Jesus is dying on the cross and says to the penitent criminal: 'Today you will be with me in Paradise.' And we have Paul's testimony that someone he knew (perhaps himself) had been carried up to the third heaven from where he had for a short time entered Paradise, again suggesting that Paul too believed that the end times had arrived.

The second topic of interest to us here is the connection between the Garden of Eden and the Temple.[4] The Garden of Eden is seen by the author of Genesis as an archetypal sanctuary, protected by the cherubim, the traditional guardians of holy places in that part of the world.[5] On top of the ark, two cherubim formed the throne of God in the inner sanctuary of the Temple, and pictures of the cherubim decorated the curtains of the Tabernacle and walls of the Temple. Detailed study by Margaret Barker has taken the connection between the Garden and the Temple further in a universal and more mystical direction. The Temple, it is argued, is a place of creation and renewal. The Temple was designed to represent the Garden of Eden. It was also built as a place of mediation and atonement with God, themes associated with the veil of the Temple, which symbolized the boundary between earth and heaven.

Furthermore, the temple is also a place where some could pass beyond the veil and experience the vision of God, seeing into the essence of things past, present and future. These are the visions of the divine throne which are best known from the Revelation of St John.[6]

Such imagery has been expressed lyrically in some well-known hymns, in which the themes of Jerusalem, Temple and the marriage of the Lamb are interwoven. While drawing directly from St John's Revelation, these images have their roots in the Song and other Wisdom writings.

> Blessed city, heavenly Salem,
> Vision dear of peace and love,
> Who of living stones upbuilded,
> Art the joy of heaven above,
> And, with angel cohorts circled,
> As a bride on earth dost move!
>
> From celestial realms descending,
> Ready for the nuptial bed,
> To his presence, decked with jewels,
> By her Lord shall she be led;
> All her streets, and all her bulwarks,
> Of pure gold are fashioned.
>
> *Urbs beata, c.* seventh century[7]

ෆෆෆෆෆෆ ✿ ෯෯෯෯෯෯

ෆ 35 ෆ

The Garden and the Temple (2)

It may well be that the Temple was deliberately built by Solomon as a garden sanctuary, in which golden palm trees and flowers, set within precious stones, were made to decorate the walls. Bronze pillars were set with pomegranate patterns, and the great lamp was a stylized almond tree. 'The "garden" was wholly within the temple, and therefore the temple *was* the garden.'[1]

The lover addresses his beloved as 'my sister, my bride', and describes her as a garden locked. So in our metaphorical understanding, the beloved is the garden – the Temple – which remains locked until the day of the Lord comes. Then it will be finally liberated.

The references to water – 'a fountain sealed', 'a well of living water, and flowing streams from Lebanon' – confirm the strong impression that the location is the Temple. The most significant text here is the description of the river of water flowing from the Temple, which we find in the prophet Ezekiel's vision of a newly restored Temple, to replace that destroyed by the Babylonians: 'Then he [the Lord] brought me back to the door of the Temple; and behold water was flowing from below the threshold of the temple . . .'[2]

For many, the heavenly Jerusalem can hardly be thought of as a place of complete and utter peace unless it also includes a garden and natural aspects of the Promised Land. In one of his best-known hymns, St Bernard of Clairvaux (Cluny) introduces the idea of 'Jerusalem the golden' being set within 'pastures of the blessed', 'decked in glorious sheen', and the city being located within 'a sweet and blessed country'.

> Jerusalem the golden
> With milk and honey blest,
> Beneath thy contemplation
> Sink heart and voice opprest.
> I know not, O I know not,
> What social joys are there,
> What radiancy of glory,
> What light beyond compare.
>
> They stand, those halls of Sion,
> Conjubilant with song,
> And bright with many an angel,
> And all the martyr throng;
> The Prince is ever in them,
> The daylight is serene,
> The pastures of the blessed,
> Are decked in glorious sheen.
>
> O sweet and blessed country,
> Shall I ever see thy face?
> O sweet and blessed country,
> Shall I ever win thy grace?
> Exult, O dust and ashes!

The Lord shall be thy part:
His only, his for ever,
Thou shalt be, and thou art![3]

C

ෲෲෲෲෲෲ ☼ ෴ෳෳෳෳෳ

ෲ 36 ෲ

The river of the water of life

The image of Ezekiel's life-giving river in a restored Temple of Jerusalem becomes a central motif in a vision of a restored Paradise in the Revelation of St John. The river of the water of life, flowing down the middle of the street in the new Jerusalem, forms a tree-lined canal.[1] Into this restored Paradise come the nations, now redeemed. The leaves of the trees are their cure. 'God's curse, pronounced over the whole of creation because of Adam's disobedience, is abrogated, for the whole creation has been renewed by the re-creating hand of God, and no flaming sword now bars the way to the tree of life.'[2]

Yet it is not only in that vision of the new Jerusalem that we find strong echoes of the Song elsewhere in Scripture. In Isaiah, the Psalms and the Gospels, water, wells and springs all have a saving connotation. 'With joy you will draw water from the wells of salvation.' 'All my springs are in you [Jerusalem].' 'With you is the well of life.'[3] Jesus promises the Samaritan woman at Jacob's well 'living water', a 'spring of water gushing up to eternal life'.[4] And, significantly, it is in the context of the Temple that Jesus cries: 'The one believing in me, as scripture has said, out of his belly will flow living water.' The phrase 'living water' there is precisely the same wording as we find here in the Greek Septuagint version of the Song.

A Jewish commentator writes:

> In this encomium, the natural springs of earthly life are metaphorically transposed on two planes: the first is the concrete temple, which is portrayed here in terms of spiritual renewal; while the second is God himself, who is presented as the fountain of all life and light. The religious depths of this imagery take us to the heart of biblical spirituality and the religious experience of the temple.[5]

O water, life-bestowing,
Forth from the Saviour's heart
A fountain purely flowing,
A fount of love thou art:
O let us, freely tasting,
Our burning thirst assuage;
Thy sweetness, never wasting,
Avails from age to age.[6]

Maintzich Gesangbuch (1661)

ᘓᘓᘓᘓᘓᘓ ✿ ᘔᘔᘔᘔᘔᘔ

ᘓ 37 ᘓ

Pomegranates and spices

4.13 Your channel is an orchard of pomegranates
        with all choicest fruits,
        henna with nard,
4.14 nard and saffron, calamus and cinnamon,
        with all trees of frankincense,
        myrrh and aloes,
        with all chief spices –
4.15 a garden fountain, a well of living water.

The word 'channel' here translates a Hebrew plural word that means
something like 'extension, limbs'.[1] Probably the line would be better
translated, 'Your limbs are a paradise of pomegranates.' Pomegranates
have an extensive background in the Holy Scriptures. Because of
their many seeds, they are an obvious symbol of fertility, although
it is their close connection with the Temple and its worship that
is of special interest to us. The Temple court itself was a 'paradise
of pomegranates'. On each of the two great pillars that stood in
the forecourt hung 200 bronze pomegranates, glittering in the
sunlight. It is likely that people viewed the pomegranates as symbols
of life.[2]

At the time of Israel's exile in Babylon, the Chaldeans smashed
up and carried away all the bronze in the temple, including the

pomegranates. Here in the Song the pomegranates are followed by a list of the spices that supplied the constituents of the holy anointing oil and the holy incense that were in regular use in the Temple.

The prophet Joel laments bitterly, mourning the loss of the land, where the living pomegranates, palm and apple and all the trees of the field are withered.[3] From this we may conclude that the poet of the Song, like Joel, saw a strong link between the prosperity of the Temple and the land. In some way, possibly originally connected with the prayers of priest and people for the fertility of the land and for the holiness of the Temple ritual, pomegranates were a symbol of the blessing of God.

There is another link between the Temple ritual and pomegranates. Moses was ordered to make for his brother Aaron, the priest, pomegranates of blue and scarlet threads around the hem of his ephod (his priestly garment), to be worn whenever he went into the holy place of the Lord.[4]

Today garments such as the surplice, stole and vestments are an obvious and outward sign of the priestly or ministerial calling. The priestly task is to act as a bridge-builder between God and humanity. This raises a question about the moral worthiness of the priest who is charged with such a momentous responsibility. Since early times it has been well understood that even if a minister is morally unworthy, this cannot nullify God's gifts of Word and Sacrament.[5] Otherwise nobody could be assured of receiving God's grace. Yet it is also true that only when Christian ministers and priests clothe themselves, or rather, are rather clothed with, the true garments of Christ, can they appear before the people with true integrity. In the poem 'Aaron', George Herbert, in keeping with his overall theme of *The Temple*, draws on the imagery of the external dress and accoutrements of the priests of ancient Israel to lead his readers into the theme of God's transforming grace, symbolized by putting on Christ, by whom alone as priest he can be 'well drest'.

Aaron

Holiness on the head,
Light and perfections on the breast,
Harmonious bells below, raising the dead
To lead them unto life and rest.
Thus are true Aarons drest.

Profaneness in my head,
Defects and darkness in my breast,
A noise of passions ringing me for dead
Unto a place where is no rest:
Poor priest! thus am I drest.

Only another head
I have, another heart and breast,
Another music, making live, not dead,
Without whom I could have no rest:
In Him I am well drest.

Christ is my only head,
My alone only heart and breast,
My only music, striking me e'en dead;
That to the old man I may rest,
And be in Him new drest.

So holy in my head,
Perfect and light in my dear breast,
My doctrine tun'd by Christ (who is not dead,
But lives in me while I do rest),
Come, people; Aaron's drest.

CRCRCRCRCRCR ☼ ဆဆဆဆဆဆ

൦ﬞ38൦ﬞ

Frustrated love

5.2 I slept, but my heart was awake.
Listen! my beloved is knocking.
'Open to me, my sister, my love,
my dove, my perfect one;
for my head is wet with dew,
my locks with the drops of the night.'
5.3 I had put off my garment;
how could I put it on again?
I had bathed my feet;
how could I soil them?

5.4 My beloved thrust his hand into the opening,
    and my inmost being yearned for him.

5.5 I arose to open to my beloved,
    and my hands dripped with myrrh,
my fingers with liquid myrrh,
    upon the handles of the bolt.

5.6 I opened to my beloved,
    but my beloved had turned and was gone.
My soul failed me when he spoke.
I sought him, but did not find him;
    I called him, but he gave me no answer.

5.7 Making their rounds in the city
    the sentinels found me;
they beat me, they wounded me,
    they took away my mantle,
    those sentinels of the walls.

5.8 I adjure you, O daughters of Jersualem,
    If you find my beloved,
tell him this:
    I am faint with love.

Love's insistence

I slept, but my heart was awake,
Listen! my beloved is knocking.
'Open to me, my sister, my love,
    my dove, my perfect one;
for my head is wet with dew,
    my locks with the drops of the night.'

The verbs here translated 'slept' and 'was awake' are actually in the present tense. So if we read the poem at a literal level, this is not a flashback to a time before the two lovers were intimate. It is a description of frustrated love, when the normal close bonds seem to be broken. The beloved bride, just described as a 'locked garden', is locked behind a door that excludes her lover. When the bridegroom puts his hand through 'the opening', by which is meant 'the keyhole – the wooden keys of antiquity were large – he is unable to slip the bolt'.[1] His beloved refuses to open the door because she has washed and is undressed. At a literal level this may be understandable. The wedding has not yet been celebrated. The bride is not ready for the consummation of the marriage. But there is more to it than inconvenience or impropriety. Her unwillingness to respond seems inexplicable in the light of her previous overwhelming longing for her lover. Our own experience, however, teaches us plenty enough about the vacillations of the human heart, which, blowing hot and cold, become obstacles to true personal commitment.

Reading this passage at the metaphorical level, we can perhaps sense that the beloved woman's failure to respond to the divine Lover's approach is a picture of the spiritual condition known variously as listlessness or acedia. Acedia (or accidie) is a state of restlessness, an inability either to work or to pray. Thomas Aquinas identified acedia with 'the sorrow of the world' – that is, 'sorrow about spiritual good in as much as it is a Divine good'.[2] It is essentially a flight from the world that leads to not caring even that one does not care. It is the opposite of the spiritual joy that comes from love.

George Herbert saw such failure as a symptom of human restlessness and lack of constancy – what he called 'giddiness'.

Giddiness

O what a thing is man! How far from power,
From set'led peace and rest!
He is some twenty sev'ral men at least
Each sev'ral hour.

One while he counts of heav'n, as of his treasure:
But then a thought creeps in,
And calls him coward, who for fear of sin
Will lose a pleasure.

He builds a house, which quickly down must go,
As if a whirlwind blew
And crusht the building: and it's partly true,
His mind is so.

Surely if each one saw another's heart,
There would be no commerce,
No sale or bargain pass: all would disperse,
And live apart.

Lord, mend or rather make us: one creation
Will not suffice our turn:
Except thou make us daily, we shall spurn
Our own salvation.[3]

ଔଔଔଔଔଔ ☼ ଷଷଷଷଷଷ

ଔ39ଔ

Heart awake

'I slept, but my heart was awake.' Teresa of Avila used this line to explain to her sisters that 'while the faculties are asleep or suspended, love remains alive', meaning that when our normal senses are put on one side for the purpose of contemplative prayer, Christ the Bridegroom supplies for the soul what the soul cannot do for itself.[1] In other words, there is a stage in the practice of contemplative prayer when the external senses become less acute, and the internal senses, such as seeing or hearing with the heart, become more awake, more alive. St Anthony of Egypt said: 'That prayer is not perfect in the course of which the monk is aware of the fact that he is praying.'[2] In other words, self-consciousness is the enemy of true prayer. If the best definition of prayer is absolute attention to God,[3] then the more deeply we are immersed, the less we are aware of our external surroundings, or distracted by internal anxieties, hopes and dreams.

The twentieth-century poet Ursula Fanthorpe used the metaphor of a house whose doors are shut to explore the idea of a communal practice of silent prayer emerging out of a steady long-term commitment to inhabit fully the present moment. But this can only happen through shutting down the senses, and the abandoning of 'lovely holy distractions, safe scaffolding of much-loved formulae', so that the 'herb of silence' can take root and grow.

> **Friends Meeting House, Frenchay, Bristol**
> When the doors of the house are shut,
> Eyes lidded, mouth closed, nose and ears
> Doing their best to idle, fingers allowed out

Only on parole, when the lovely holy distractions,
Safe scaffolding of much-loved formulae,
Have been rubbed away; then the plant
Begins to grow. It is hard to rear,
Rare herb of silence, through which the Word comes,
Three centuries of reticent, meticulous lives
Have naturalised it to the ground.[4]

CRCRCRCRCRCR ☼ ꙮꙮꙮꙮꙮꙮ

⊛ 40 ⊛

The broken connection

5.4 My beloved thrust his hand into the opening,
    and my inmost being yearned for him.
5.5 I arose to open to my beloved,
    and my hands dripped with myrrh,
  my fingers with liquid myrrh,
    upon the handles of the bolt.
5.6 I opened to my beloved,
    but my beloved had turned and was gone.
  My soul failed me when he spoke.
  I sought him, but did not find him;
    I called him, but he gave me no answer.

'And my guts heaved/churned for him' is a literal translation of the second line in verse 4. For Jewish readers it would probably have brought to mind the very similar words of God's lament over the loss of Ephraim, the Northern Kingdom, when it was destroyed by the Assyrians. 'Is Ephraim my dear son – a dandled child? As often as I speak against him, surely I remember him still. Therefore do my guts heave/churn for him; surely I will have mercy upon him, says the LORD.'[1] During the Babylonian exile, two centuries after the Assyrian invasion, these words came to Jeremiah from the Lord as a message of hope and assurance. And we find a very similar expression when another prophet of the same period boldly reproaches God for delaying the restoration of Israel to their land. 'Where is the churning of your guts for Israel?'[2] It seems as if Israel's prophets had no difficulty in ascribing to God a visceral attachment to his people, one reciprocated by Israel, who here laments, 'My soul failed me when he spoke.' This is like saying, 'I almost died' (from the unbearable pain of having heard but not having responded).

Further hints that this is an encounter with a divine Lover are suggested by the two references to myrrh in verse 5. Myrrh, as already mentioned, is the chief ingredient of the 'holy anointing oil' with which the priests and the sanctuary of the Temple were anointed.[3] And for us myrrh has, of course, unforgettable associations with the Messiah whose death is prefigured by the gift of myrrh, and who was indeed anointed with myrrh for burial. So myrrh is doubly holy.

 CЯCЯCЯCЯCЯCЯCЯ ☼ Ю Я ЮЯ ЮЯ ЮЯ ЮЯ ЮЯ

ℭℨ*41*ℭℨ

The wounded lover[1]

> 5.7   Making their rounds in the city
>   the sentinels found me;
>   they beat me, they wounded me,
>   they took away my mantle,
>   those sentinels of the walls.

The poem now takes an unexpectedly dark and violent turn. The bride is attacked and wounded by the city guards, whom she had previously questioned as to her lover's whereabouts. It is not clear why they now abuse her. Maybe they see her as defying the social mores. In ancient societies, and indeed in some contemporary cultures, young unmarried women are supposed to stay at home, and when they go out of doors are accompanied by an escort. Are they treating her as they might a prostitute, stripping her of her outer clothing? Reading the poem at a literal level, the commentators are baffled.

One way of understanding this incident is to see it as relating to two kinds of spiritual experience to which the Song is pointing. The city appears symbolically in some parts of the Song as the sphere of separation and suffering, whereas the garden represents that which brings satisfaction, delight and union. 'Garden and city represent the two faces of Jerusalem as it appears in the Bible, positive and negative respectively.'[2] On the one hand, Jerusalem and its Temple, as we have seen, are celebrated by the psalmists and prophets as the place for intimate meeting between God and his people. On the other, it is called 'the city of blood',[3] or the city that 'sinned grievously'.[4] Jesus accuses Jerusalem of being the city that kills prophets and stones those who are sent to it.[5] And we see both aspects of Jerusalem coming to the fore in the story and suffering of Jesus, who would certainly have prayed with the psalmist for the peace of Jerusalem. The poet maybe has in mind the psalmist's lament for the treachery of his 'companion', his one-time 'familiar friend': 'I see violence and strife in the city. Day and night they go around it on its walls, and iniquity and trouble are within it; ruin is in its midst.'[6]

We return again to the mystery of the wounded lover.[7] If the mantle or veil in verse 7 represents the beloved's last defence before surrendering herself to the full embrace of her divine Lover, then in contemporary terms we could identify it as a covering that must be removed, as the last defence of the ego that hinders perfect union with God. The sentinels or watchmen of the city may thus be interpreted as God's angels, or agents of 'tough love' who painfully strip away the beloved's illusions, or those parts of her/us that remain stubbornly resistant to the necessary work of purification.

We find perhaps the most subtle and beautiful commentary on the intimate relationship between 'Love' and the beloved guest, and the obstacles of shame, guilt and pride that need to be overcome, in the culminating poem of George Herbert's collection *The Temple*. In 12 intense lines of dialogue, Love breaks down one by one the barriers erected by the guest's feelings of unworthiness, fear and stubborn egotism. The guest is gently reminded how Love itself took the blame for human sin, and the door is open for the guest to sit down to eat with his host.

Love III

Love bade me welcome, yet my soul drew back,
    Guilty of dust and sin.
But quick-ey'd Love, observing me grow slack
    From my first entrance in,

Drew nearer to me, sweetly questioning
   If I lack'd anything.

'A guest,' I answer'd, 'worthy to be here';
   Love said, 'You shall be he.'
'I, the unkind, the ungrateful? ah my dear,
   I cannot look on thee.'
Love took my hand and smiling did reply,
   'Who made the eyes but I?'

'Truth, Lord, but I have marr'd them; let my shame
   Go where it doth deserve.'
'And know you not,' says Love, 'who bore the blame?'
   'My dear, then I will serve.'
'You must sit down,' says Love, 'and taste my meat.'
   So I did sit and eat.

ങ ങ ങ ങ ങ ങ ✿ ബ ബ ബ ബ ബ ബ

ങ *42* ങ

Reunion

6.3   I am my beloved's and my beloved is mine.

(See Chapter 2 for a commentary on the love song of 5.10—16.)

The verse in Hebrew expresses the mutual and exclusive love between the couple in just four words. They could equally well be translated, 'I am for my lover, and my lover is for me', which expresses something more than an exclusive attachment, but rather a commitment to seek the well-being of the other. So this assertion of love embraces both *eros* (passion) and, in New Testament terms, *agape* (self-giving love). Such mutual avowal is popular among contemporary Israeli young people. The Hebrew words 'are cast in gold and silver and worn as pendants and rings. Young lovers think of this, quite rightly, as the biblical love slogan. Wearing it they anchor their own fresh experience in the tradition.'[1] But the tradition is as long as the covenant made between God and the Israelite people on Mount Sinai, where it was proclaimed: 'I will walk among you, and will be your God, and you shall be my people.'[2]

Interestingly, a definite connection between the commitment made by the lovers in the Song and the covenant made at Sinai was common among the rabbis of old. Rabbi Akiva told the following story.[3]

> All the nations of the world came to ask the same question asked by the daughters of Jerusalem.[4] 'What is so special about your beloved, your God, that you are willing even to suffer and to die for him?' Israel is incredulous at their ignorance. 'Do you know him? We will tell you just a little of his praise. 'My beloved is all radiant and ruddy . . .'[5] After hearing this song of praise, the nations, like the daughters of Jerusalem, are eager to join Israel in seeking Israel's lover, but unfortunately they cannot be included.

According to the rabbi's story, God's love is exclusive. The relationship is not available to those who seek God *as just one possible option*. Only those who commit themselves fully are vindicated in their faith.

In his little book *The Epistle of Prayer*, the anonymous fourteenth-century author of *The Cloud of Unknowing* comments on this verse: 'you will be united and spiritually secured by grace on his [God's] part, and by a loving consent and glad spirit on yours'.[6] The writer hits the nail on the head. In one sense all depends upon God's grace. At the same time, there is no compulsion. Free and loving consent is necessary on our part. The fruit of this spiritual marriage is a unity that is not temporary or passing, but entirely secure, for God is to be trusted, and his love unconditional.

St Augustine expresses in his *Confessions* his belated discovery of God's love. Or rather, as it seemed to him, God broke through his deafness and blindness to reveal himself not as outside his soul, as he had imagined, but already within him. The images that he uses noticeably echo the erotic flavour of the language of the Song, especially references to God's beauty, fragrance and taste.

> Late have I loved Thee, O Beauty so ancient and so new; late have I loved Thee! For behold Thou wert within me, and I outside; and I sought Thee outside and in my unloveliness fell upon

those lovely things that Thou hast made. Thou wert with me and I was not with Thee. I was kept from Thee by these things, yet had they not been in Thee, they would not have been at all. Thou didst call and cry to me and break open my deafness; and Thou didst send forth Thy beams and shine upon me and chase away my blindness. Thou didst breathe fragrance upon me, and I drew in my breath and do now pant for Thee: I tasted Thee, and now hunger and thirst for Thee: Thou didst touch me, and I have burned for Thy peace.[7]

ઝ ઝ ઝ ઝ ઝ ઝ ✿ ຂ ຂ ຂ ຂ ຂ ຂ

ઝ 43 ઝ

God's assurance and care

> 6.13   Return, return, O Shulammite!
>   Return, return, that we may look upon you.
>
>   Why should you look upon the Shulammite,
>   as upon a dance before two armies?

(For a commentary on the love song in 6.13—7.9 see Chapter 2.)

The term 'Shulammite' is never explained, and it does not appear anywhere else in the Scriptures. It looks like a word derived from the name of a place (formed like 'the Shunammite woman' from the town of Shunem).[1] However, there is no known place called 'Shulam', nor is it a name used elsewhere in the Bible. It may possibly have been invented or imagined by the poet, and refer to Zion, otherwise known as 'Salem' (Hebrew *Shalem*), in which case the woman symbolizes Jerusalem, the object of God's love. The 'dance before two armies' could refer to the two kingdoms of Israel and Judah, Northern and Southern, that split after Solomon's death.

There is another possibility. The root consonants of Shulammite are *sh-l-m*, suggesting *shalom* – peace. If the name Jerusalem (in Hebrew, *Yerushalayim*) means foundation of peace, then there is an association between the woman and peace. So 'the Shulammite' is the female counterpart of Solomon (Hebrew *Shlomo*), but without the chequered history of Solomon, whose religious inconsistency was believed to be the cause of the split between north and south. By contrast, the Shulammite woman embodies a peace that reunites north and south.

At a personal level, the Shulammite woman may also then be seen as an archetype of a soul at peace with God.

As for the repeated 'return', again we seem to hear an echo of Jeremiah 31, where, significantly, Israel is also viewed as a young and beloved woman. Twice she is called to return home: 'Return, O virgin Israel, return to these your cities.'[2]

> The days are surely coming, says the LORD, when I will make a new covenant with the house of Israel and the house of Judah. It will not be like the covenant that I made with their ancestors when I took them by the hand to bring them out of the land of Egypt – a covenant that they broke, though I was their husband, says the LORD.[3]

It is important to notice that the repeated call, 'return', is based on the promise that despite Israel's faithlessness, God, her disappointed 'husband', continues to love and care for her.

Once again we get this composite picture of a young woman who collectively symbolizes Jerusalem or Israel, and individually the soul of the woman who, despite her struggles with sin and failure, still desires to return to her divine Lover. George Herbert expresses the response of the Christian soul to the resurrection of Jesus in the ecstasy of Easter joy, in his play on the image of the Sun (Son). There is perhaps also an allusion to the Song in the reference to highly valued Eastern perfume.

> **Easter II**
> I got me flowers to straw thy way;
> I got me boughs off many a tree:
> But thou wast up by break of day,
> And brought'st thy sweets along with thee.
>
> The Sun arising in the East,
> Though he give light, and th'East perfume;
> If they should offer to contest
> With thy arising, they presume.

Can there be any day but this,
Though many suns to shine endeavour?
We count three hundred, but we miss:
there is but one, and that one ever.

ඦඦඦඦඦඦ ✿ ඩඩඩඩඩඩ

ඦ44ඦ

His desire is for me

> 7.10   I am my beloved's,
>   and his desire is for me.

Here the bride states for the third time the phrase that sums up their mutual devotion, but this time with a significant change. The new word is 'desire', and it stands out because it is rare, occurring elsewhere in the Hebrew Scriptures only in the Genesis story of the Garden of Eden, and following that, in the story of Cain and Abel.

> To the woman [God] said, 'I will greatly increase your pangs in childbearing; in pain you shall bring forth children, yet your desire shall be for your husband, and he shall rule over you.'[1]

Here in the Song the situation is reversed. No longer is the woman's desire for her husband spoken of, but rather 'his desire for her'. The divine Lover loves his beloved with a burning and longing intensity.

In the context of both the Hebrew Scriptures and the New Testament, this is highly significant. At a literal level, the woman and man meet here in full equality of both power and desire. There is no hint of subjugation, inferior status or male headship. So the Song reinstates woman's original place as a *partner* absolutely equal to her husband.[2]

Reading the Song metaphorically, it is also implied that the estrangement between humanity and God has been put right. Turning to the story of Cain and Abel, we find the second appearance of the word 'desire'. When God sees Cain's growing anger towards his brother, he warns him: 'sin is lurking at the door; its desire is for you, but you must master it'. Sin is not simply a word for human frailty; it is a destructive force that can rise up, strike us down and enslave us.[3] St Peter describes the devil as like a roaring lion, seeking whom he may devour, eager to find weaknesses. But the good news is this. However eagerly sin lurks to catch and destroy us, the desire of the divine Lover to hold us in his embrace is greater. In his commentary on the Gospel story of the Samaritan woman at the well, St Augustine expresses the truth like this: 'He asks for a drink, and he promises a drink. He is in need as one who is going to receive; and he is rich as one who is going to satisfy.'[4]

William H. Vanstone (1923–99) expressed something of this burning and poignant love of Christ in a remarkable hymn reflecting something of his own experience of more than 20 years of pastoral work in a Lancashire housing estate, about which he wrote in a prize-winning book of the same name.

> **Love's endeavour, love's expense**
> Drained is love in making full,
> bound in setting others free,
> poor in making others rich
> weak in giving power to be.
>
> Therefore he who shows us God
> helpless hangs upon the tree;
> and the nails and crown of thorns
> tell of what God's love must be.
>
> Here is God: no monarch he,
> throne in easy state to reign;
> here is God, whose arms of love
> aching, spent, the world sustain.[5]

Nothing else but God's intense inexhaustible desire for humanity makes sense of the biblical story, from the calling of Abraham to the Incarnation of God in Christ, even to Jesus' death nailed to a cross.[6]

The thirteenth-century mystic Mechthild of Magdeburg expresses her ecstatic delight in God's inexhaustible love for humanity:

God's desire and the soul's ecstatic response
O God, you pour yourself in your gift!
O God, you run down in your love!
O God, you burn with desire!
O God, you melt in the union with your loved one!
O God, you live at rest between my breasts,
without you I cannot live![7]

ଔଔଔଔଔଔ ✿ ଔଔଔଔଔଔ

ଔ 45 ଔ

Continuing desire for union

8.1 O that you were like a brother to me,
who nursed at my mother's breast!
If I met you outside, I would kiss you,
and no one would despise me.

8.2 I would lead you and bring you
into the house of my mother,
and into the chamber of the one who bore me.
I would give you spiced wine to drink,
the juice of my pomegranates.

8.3 O that his left hand were under my head,
and that his right hand embraced me!

8.4 I adjure you, O daughters of Jerusalem,
do not stir up or awaken love
until it is ready!

If taken literally, the woman's cautious words here are hardly consistent with the unconventional attitude to social mores that she shows earlier.[1] In such a culture (as in many non-Western contemporary cultures) a woman could not kiss a man publicly unless he was known to be a close blood relation, such as a brother or brother's son. The Targum interprets this verse metaphorically as alluding to the future day when the Messiah will come and be invited to be like a brother to his bride Israel, and they will go up to Jerusalem together and 'suck the judgements of the Torah'.[2]

It is perhaps best to read these verses, including verse 3, as an expression of the continuing desire of the beloved to be united to her lover in the most intimate embrace. The reference to kissing outside in the street reverses the unfortunate situation described in Proverbs,[3] where the seductress Lady Folly is seen likewise outside in the street. Seizing the unwary young man she kisses him, and brings upon him shame and humiliation. Here the bride, signifying Lady Wisdom, declares she would indeed kiss her Lover publicly, and she would not be despised for it. Being God's 'consort', Wisdom is entitled to express her love for God openly and freely.

The references to 'house' and 'mother' point allegorically to the Temple. 'Spiced wine' is found only here in the Hebrew Bible, and connects with the instructions for the preparation of the holy anointing oil, in which are mixed myrrh, cassia and oil, used in the Temple.[4] As already noted, pomegranates also suggest the Temple.[5] The oil was used to anoint the tent of meeting, the ark of the covenant and the altar, all being symbols of God's intimacy with his people. So these verses allude to both Wisdom and the Temple which, as we recall, are closely linked.

(Verses 8.3 and 8.4 virtually repeat 2.6, 2.7 and 3.5. See the commentary on those verses above.)

ꙄꙄꙄꙄꙄꙄ ☼ ꙅꙅꙅꙅꙅꙅ

Ꙅ46ꙅ

Devoted bride

> 8.5 Who is that coming up from the wilderness,
> leaning upon her beloved?

The first half of 8.5 is identical to 3.6, whereas in the second half the phrase, 'leaning upon her beloved' replaces 'like a column of smoke', but the interpretation of the two verses is complementary. The earlier verse suggests the desert, the smoke of incense and the ark of the covenant, symbolized by the royal litter. The second suggests the dependence of the bride upon her Lover. Jeremiah writes that the Lord declared to his bride Israel: 'I remember the devotion of your youth, your love as a bride, how you followed me in the wilderness, in a land not sown.'[1] The prophet's witness applies to both verses.

In his commentary on the Song St Bernard of Clairvaux writes: 'all the bride's efforts are in vain if she does not lean on God. When the bride does trust in God she will acquire new resources in herself, become stronger and be able to subordinate everything else to reason.' He quotes Philippians 4.3: 'I can do everything through him who gives me strength'; Mark 9.23: 'Everything is possible for him who believes'; and James 1.15: 'If any of you lacks wisdom he should ask of God, who gives generously to all without finding fault.'

C３C３C３C３C３C３ ☼ ８０８０８０８０８０８０

C３ 47 C３

The infinite power of love

> 8.6 Set me as a seal upon your heart,
>   as a seal upon your arm;
> for love is strong as death,
>   passion fierce as the grave.
> Its flashes are flashes of fire,
>   a raging flame.
> 8.7 Many waters cannot quench love,
>   neither can floods drown it.
> If one offered for love
>   all the wealth of his house,
>   it would be utterly scorned.

A seal upon your heart

In the world of the Song, as indeed in many ancient cultures, personal seals were often worn on cords around the neck or the arm. The seal was like a personal signature. It marked a person's word as binding, and provided evidence of honesty and integrity in one's dealings.

It is possible, however, that this seal may mean more than a personal signature. When the people went into exile to Babylon, the prophet Jeremiah wrote these words: 'As I live, says the LORD, even if King Coniah . . . were the signet ring on my right hand, even from there I would tear you off and give you into the hands of . . . King Nebuchadrezzar.'[1] God has worn Israel's anointed king like 'a seal ring'. He is now threatening to tear it off, because of the moral degeneration of both king and people.

Here again in the Song there is a reversal of a dire prophecy. The implication of 'Set me as a seal upon your heart' could be that now it is time for God to put on a new signet, a new sign of commitment. That this interpretation is likely is supported by God's promise to King Zerubbabel during the time of restoration after the Exile: 'I will take you, O Zerubbabel my servant . . . and make you like a signet ring; for I have chosen you, says the LORD of hosts.'[2]

If indeed the bride symbolizes both Wisdom and Jerusalem, and the city herself as a unified people under God, and also the individual soul intimately united with God, the seal 'serves as a "stamp" of God's identity'.[3] The seal is thus a verification of God's loving purposes towards the world. Ellen Davis raises an existential question: does the image of the seal indicate that love itself stands as a kind of protection against what we most fear, our own extinction? Do we fear that our identity will be snuffed out, that all we do and strive for in life counts for nothing?

In St John's Revelation, the risen and ascended Christ makes promises of life to each of the Seven Churches of Asia. To the church at Pergamum he declares: 'To everyone who conquers I will give some of the hidden manna, and I will give a white stone, and on the white stone is written a new name that no one knows except the one who receives it.'[4]

According to rabbinic legend, the manna given in the wilderness was preserved in a golden jar in the Holy of Holies, and then hidden by Jeremiah at the destruction of the Temple in 586 BCE. The legend predicted that the manna would reappear at the coming of the Messiah. The white stone or pebble may thus be a symbol of admission to the heavenly banquet, won for each of the redeemed by the Victor's conquest of sin and death. This stone bears the secret name of Jesus Christ, which no one can learn except by sharing in his suffering.[5]

CRCRCRCRCRCR ✿ ♌♌♌♌♌♌

ᓍ 48 ᓍ

Strong as death

> 8.6 for love is strong as death,
> passion fierce as the grave.
> Its flashes are flashes of fire,
> a raging flame.

These are the best-known lines in the whole poem. As Ellen Davis points out, 'This is the only "objective" statement in the whole poem about the supreme value of love.'[1] While the rest of the poem is largely taken up with the two lovers' words to one another, 'the tone here is magisterial, the claim sweeping'.[2] They are echoed in a modern eucharistic liturgy, in which it is proclaimed that 'he [Christ] offered his life for sinners, and with a love stronger than death opened his arms on the cross'.[3] So death does not have the last word, but in accordance with the prophetic promise 'has been swallowed up in victory', the victory of Christ's resurrection.[4] 'So love is the first and last gift of God, which cannot be destroyed by death.'[5]

But how does love resemble death? Because it *may* consume us in this life – if we allow it – as fully as death *will* certainly consume us. For those who yield to it, love does indeed consume like 'a raging flame'. But in this image there is also a no doubt deliberate echo of the biblical image of God as 'a devouring or consuming fire', to be found in both the Old and New Testaments: 'For the LORD your God is a devouring fire'; 'let us give thanks, by which we offer to God an acceptable worship with reverence and awe; for indeed our God is a consuming fire.'[6] A consuming fire destroys what is useless, burns the dross, and refines what has to be cleansed, but also symbolizes the purity and power of love.

A fifteenth-century Christian prayer, adapted as a hymn for Pentecost, takes this image of a raging flame to describe the work of God's love in the human soul:

> Come down, O Love divine,
> Seek thou this soul of mine,
> And visit it with thine own ardour glowing;
> O Comforter, draw near,

Within my heart appear,
And kindle it, thy holy flame bestowing.[7]

Bianca da Siena (d. 1434)

CRCRCRCRCRCR ✿ ಜಜಜಜಜಜ

ଓଃ*49*ଓଃ

Jealous love

8.6   . . . passion fierce as the grave.

The Hebrew word here translated as 'fierce' is more accurately rendered as 'jealous'. Jealousy is generally thought of negatively, a symptom of a possessive and unhealthy love. But here it describes the kind of single-minded love that is unwaveringly focused on just one person and expects the same response from the beloved. Jealousy can then be seen positively as a constant and unwavering readiness to defend what is weak or vulnerable. It may be seen, perhaps, in a parent's passionate desire to defend their child from death or injury, and willingness to risk life and limb to do so, or in someone who goes to protect a stranger suffering abuse or injury. Such examples may give us a model of how God loves Israel with a unique passion, a burning jealous love, that will never be compromised. The poet of the Song could well be drawing upon the words of the post-exilic prophet Zechariah: 'Thus says the LORD of Hosts, I am very jealous for Jerusalem and for Zion.' Jerusalem and its Temple are to be rebuilt for the returning exiles, and then 'I will be a wall of fire all round it, says the LORD.'[1]

Jean Vanier is a French-Canadian who founded the movement known as L'Arche, a federation of about 130 residential communities around the world. The movement began in 1964 and is both ecumenical and inter-faith, independent of any Christian denomination, but founded on profound Christian principles.

The basic pattern of each community consists of a household in which people with learning disabilities live together with assistants. Those with learning disabilities are the core members. The communities have been accurately described as schools of desire and wisdom.

This is how David Ford, one of Britain's leading theologians, describes the significance of L'Arche:

> God desires a relationship with us for our own sake and for this to be reciprocal. We are created in God's image, the image of a God who loves us for our own sake. We are fully ourselves as we are loved for our own sake and as we love God and others for their own sakes. L'Arche seeks to be a sign of this humanity and this God. The poor, the despised, the disfigured, the disabled are especially suited to being at the heart of such a sign. There is little worldly incentive to embrace them in love and friendship, yet their deepest secret is that they are created, chosen and delighted in by God for their own sake.[2]

It is no accident that the Song of Songs is seen by Ford and other leading exponents of the Scriptures as of central significance for Christians living in the twenty-first century.

> The Song is an exclamatory poem, almost pure crying out. It is a drama of desire expressed in passionate cries, and its wisdom is a wisdom of cries. To read, re-read and internalize the Song is to find a textbook for the school of desire and wisdom, inspiring and instructing the heart and mind in attention to cries and in the articulation of cries. It may or may not be that the reader has a human lover, but the divine lover is not similarly contingent. The alertness and articulateness that may be learnt through the Song are core practices in relating to God. The cries of love are an opening up to receive love and its wisdom, a training in active receptivity.[3]

CR CR CR CR CR CR ✿ BU BU BU BU BU BU

CR 50 CR

Farewell

8.13   O you who dwell in the gardens,
        my companions are listening for your voice;
        let me hear it.

8.14 Make haste, my beloved,
     and be like a gazelle
    or a young stag
     upon the mountains of spices.

The Song finishes abruptly, just as it began. It does not end with the two lovers happily sitting together in the garden. They are still on the move. 'Make haste' may more accurately be translated as 'Flee!' So the poem ends on a note of separation and uncertainty. Is that a satisfactory conclusion? Some think not and are of the opinion that the poem should have closed with the climactic statement of the power of love in verses 6 and 7. But what we have is actually a more realistic picture of the vicissitudes of love than any fairytale idyll. The spiritual journey is not completed until death, and may possibly continue in some way beyond our imagination the other side of the grave.

The Song presents a realistic picture of our relationship with God. As the poets, the Scriptures, and the mystics alike testify, no matter how much happiness we may be fortunate enough to enjoy in this life, this world can never fully satisfy us. There has to be something more, or rather Someone more, an eternal Being who made us, loves us and redeems us by his passionate and self-giving love, drawing us into union with him. As Augustine writes: 'You have made us for yourself, O Lord, and our heart is restless until it rests in you.'[1] And according to Blaise Pascal: 'There is a God shaped vacuum in the heart of every man which cannot be filled by any created thing, but only by God, the Creator, made known through Jesus.'[2]

God reaches out to stretch and expand our desire towards heaven. We desire God only because God first desires us, and plants within us the seed of love.

One final thought. In the mysterious words 'the land of spices; something understood', the last line of George Herbert's well-known poem 'Prayer I', there may be an allusion to this final line of the Song. Herbert echoes the divine invitation to share in that most perfect prayer of all: the prayer of stillness and silence, the eternal contemplative prayer of Jesus.

Prayer I
Prayer the church's banquet, angel's age,
God's breath in man returning to his birth,

The soul in paraphrase, heart in pilgrimage,
The Christian plummet sounding heav'n and earth
Engine against th' Almighty, sinner's tow'r,
Reversed thunder, Christ-side-piercing spear,
The six-days world transposing in an hour,
A kind of tune, which all things hear and fear;
Softness, and peace, and joy, and love, and bliss,
Exalted manna, gladness of the best,
Heaven in ordinary, man well drest,
The milky way, the bird of Paradise,
Church-bells beyond the stars heard, the soul's blood,
The land of spices; something understood.

Appendix
Lectio divina *(divine reading)*

The aim of *lectio* is to move into the depths of silence and stillness where we can hear the Word spoken to us in love, and respond to this Word with our love and with our life. There are four stages or movements: reading, reflecting, praying with the mind, and praying in the heart.

Reading (lectio)
Slowly begin reading a biblical passage as if it were a long-awaited love letter addressed to you. Approach it reverentially and expectantly, in a way that 'tastes' each word and phrase. Read the passage until you hear a word or phrase that touches you, resonates, attracts or even disturbs you.

Reflecting (meditatio)
Ponder this word or phrase for a few minutes. Let it sink in slowly and deeply until you are resting in it. Listen for what the word or phrase is saying to you at this moment in your life, what it may be offering to you, what it may be demanding of you.

Praying with the mind (oratio)
When you are ready, openly and honestly express to God the prayers that arise spontaneously within you from your experience of this word or phrase. These may be prayers of thanksgiving, petition, intercession, lament or praise.

Praying in the heart (contemplatio)
Allow yourself to simply rest silently for a time in the stillness of your heart, remaining open to the quiet fullness of God's love and peace. This is like the silence of communion between a mother holding her sleeping infant child or between lovers whose communication with each other passes beyond words.

The four movements of *lectio divina* may not always follow directly one after the other. Allow yourself freedom. *Lectio* is a gentle invitation into a movement from silence into the Word and back into silence, dwelling there in the presence of God.

Notes

Introduction

1 In the Jerusalem Bible, it comes immediately before the Book of Wisdom (Ecclesiasticus).
2 It is only read regularly in religious communities.
3 Song 2.16; 6.3; No. 1 of Benjamin Britten's *Five Canticles*.
4 Information from the 'Song of Songs' article on Wikipedia (accessed 19 January 2012).
5 St Benedict of Nursia, the Father of Western Monasticism, 480–547 CE.
6 Carol Ann Duffy, poet laureate, in an article written for St Valentine's Day 2010. See <www.telegraph.co.uk/culture/books/7213958/Carol-Ann-Duffy.html>.

1 'My beloved is mine and I am his': a poem of many meanings

1 The feast of Purim.
2 One interesting exception is the distinguished Hebrew scholar Chaim Rabin of the Hebrew University. Citing concrete evidence that there were commercial and cultural contacts between Mesopotamia and the Indus civilization at the time of Solomon, he believes that there are features in the Song that have unique parallels in Tamil literature, but nowhere else in oriental love poetry. See Marvin H. Pope, *Song of Songs: A New Translation with Introduction and Commentary*, New York: Yale University Press, 1977, pp. 27ff.
3 The full titles of the following Wisdom books are: The Proverbs of Solomon son of David, king of Israel; Ecclesiastes: The words of the Teacher, the son of David, king in Jerusalem; The Wisdom of Solomon. Apart from Job and the Psalms, only Ecclesiasticus, or The Wisdom of Jesus son of Sirach stands outside the convention of linking Solomon's name to the Wisdom books.
4 The Hebrew Scriptures, translated into Greek (the Septuagint), were also added to the Christian Scriptures. These books are known by some parts of the Church as the Apocrypha, and are not regarded as having an authority equal to the books of the Old Testament. They include The Wisdom of Solomon and Sirach.
5 Stephen Mitchell, in the Foreword to *The Song of Songs: The World's First Great Love Poem*, trans. Chana Bloch and Ariel Bloch, New York: Random House, 2006, p. 3.

6 The pioneering feminist theologian Phyllis Trible argued that the rupture between man and woman in the Garden of Eden is at least part of what is being healed in the Song.

7 Cheryl Exum, *Song of Songs: A Commentary*, Louisville, KY: Westminster John Knox Press, 2005, p. 1.

8 Origen of Alexandria (*c*.184–253).

9 Denys Turner, *Eros and Allegory: Medieval Exegesis of the Song of Songs*, Kalamazoo, MI: Cistercian Publications, 1995, pp. 110–11.

10 Trevor Dennis, *Sarah Laughed: Women's Voices in the Old Testament*, London: SPCK, 1994, p. 2.

11 Adrian Thatcher, *Marriage after Modernity: Christian Marriage in Postmodern Times*, Sheffield: Sheffield Academic Press, 1999, pp. 101–2.

12 Dennis, *Sarah Laughed*, p. 2.

13 1 John 4.16.

14 St Irenaeus, Bishop of Lyons, died about 202 CE; *Against Heresies*, Book 4.20.5–7.

15 1 John 4.10, 12.

16 *New English Hymnal*, 86.

17 John Main OSB (1926–82), *Monastery Without Walls: The Spiritual Letters of John Main*, ed. Laurence Freeman, London: Canterbury Press, 2006, p. 51.

2 'O God, you burn with desire': the language of the mystic

1 Robert Burns.

2 Shakespeare, *Sonnet* 28.

3 See Graeme Watson, 'Poetry and Prayer Beyond Words', *The Way*, vol. 46 no. 1, January 2007, p. 43. I am indebted for the ideas in this paragraph to William Countryman, *The Poetic Imagination*, London: Darton, Longman and Todd, 1999.

4 Song 4.1–8.

5 Song 5.10–16.

6 Song 6.13a; 7.1–9.

7 See Ellen F. Davis, *Proverbs, Ecclesiastes, and the Song of Songs*, Louisville, KY: Westminster John Knox Press, 2000, pp. 263ff.

8 Song 4.1–3; 5.1.

9 Song 4.1.

10 See Davis, *Proverbs, Ecclesiastes, and the Song of Songs*, p. 264.

11 Song 4.6.

12 Song 3.6; 4.13–14; 5.1, 5.

13 Song 5.10–16.

14 Davis, *Proverbs, Ecclesiastes, and the Song of Songs*, p. 282.

15 Davis, *Proverbs, Ecclesiastes, and the Song of Songs*, pp. 282–3.

16 Song 6.13.

17 Gen. 14.18; Ps. 76.2. See Part 2, Song 6.13ff.

18 Ps. 48.2.

19 Ps. 122.6–8.

20 Ps. 48.1–2, 9–14; cf. Pss. 24, 48, 76, 84, 97, 122.

21 Eph. 2.4–6; cf. Eph. 1.3–14, 15–22; 3.7–10; 1 Cor. 12.4–13; Col. 1.11–13.

22 1 Cor. 3.16.

23 Source unknown.

3 'O loving wisdom of our God': a book of holy wisdom

1 David F. Ford, *Christian Wisdom: Desiring God and Learning in Love*, Cambridge: Cambridge University Press, 2007, p. 1.

2 Ford, *Christian Wisdom*, p. 1.

3 The commonly called books of Wisdom comprise Job, Psalms, Proverbs, Ecclesiastes, Song of Songs, Wisdom of Solomon, Ecclesiasticus (the Wisdom of Jesus Son of Sirach). The last two books are printed as Apocryphal or Deuterocanonical in the NRSV, but are included in the Roman Catholic, Greek and Slavonic Bibles.

4 Rabbi Akiva, *c*.135 CE.

5 See Chapter 1, p. 4.

6 Ellen F. Davis, *Proverbs, Ecclesiastes, and the Song of Songs*, Louisville, KY: Westminster John Knox Press, 2000, pp. 239–40.

7 Prov. 5.18–19.

8 Song 4.12; 2.7 and 3.5; 7.3; 1.2.

9 Wisd. 8.2.

10 Sirach 15.2.

11 Song 2.7; 3.5.

12 Song 2.7; 3.5.

13 See Edmée Kingsmill SLG, *The Song of Songs and the Eros of God*, Oxford: Oxford University Press, 2009, p. 56.

14 Prov. 7.6–23, phrases from the translation by Kingsmill in *Song of Songs*.

15 Song 3.1–4; 4.14.

16 See Part 2, Song 3.1–5.

17 Sirach 14.20–27. Gerhard von Rad, *Wisdom in Israel*, trans. James D. Martin, London: SCM Press, 1972, quoted by Kingsmill, *Song of Songs*, p. 48.

18 Song 2.9.

19 Sirach 15.2, 6; cf. Prov. 5.18.

20 Song 3.11.

21 Gerald Sheppard, *Wisdom as a Hermeneutical Construct*, New York: Walter de Gruyter, 1980, p. 53, quoted in Kingsmill, *Song of Songs*, p. 52.

22 See Kingsmill, *Song of Songs*, pp. 61ff.

23 Isa. 7.15.

24 Song 1.2, 4.

25 Song 2.4.

26 Song 4.10, translation by Kingsmill in *Song of Songs*.

27 Song 5.1.

28 Song 4.11.

29 See Kingsmill, *Song of Songs*, throughout for a detailed analysis of cross-references.

30 R. Bloch, 'Midrash', in W. S. Green (ed.), *Approaches to Ancient Judaism*, Vol. 1, Missoula, MT: Scholars Press, 1978, p. 41.

31 Davis, *Proverbs, Ecclesiastes, and the Song of Songs*, p. 41.

32 John 4.23.

33 The title 'The Temple' was probably added by Herbert's friend and editor, Nicholas Ferrar. Some of Herbert's poems are quoted in Part 2.

34 See below, 'Metaphor and allegory'.

35 George Herbert, *The Temple: Sacred Poems and Private Ejaculations*, ed. John N. Wall, Jr, New York: Paulist Press, 1981. See especially the Introduction, pp. 35ff. All Herbert's poems quoted in this book are taken from this edition.

36 Ford, *Christian Wisdom*, pp. 3–4.

37 H. W. Fowler, *Dictionary of Modern English Usage*, Oxford: Oxford University Press, 1950, p. 598.

38 John Barton, 'On the Canonicity of Canticles', in Anselm Hagerdorn (ed.), *Perspectives on the Song of Songs*, Berlin: Walter de Gruyter, 2005, quoted in Kingsmill, *Song of Songs*, p. 13.

39 Mark 4.10ff. (explicit); Matt. 21.33ff. (implicit); Gal. 4.21–31; 1 Cor. 10.1–4.

4 'God unknown, he alone calls my heart': the mystical tradition

1 Walter Brueggemann, *Theology of the Old Testament*, Minneapolis, MN: Augsburg Fortress Press, 1997, p. 417.

2 Brueggemann, *Theology of the Old Testament*, p. 417. The Hebrew word is *hsq* in Deut. 7.7, and Deut 10.15 is translated in NRSV as 'set his heart on you'.

3 Brueggemann, *Theology of the Old Testament*, p. 417.

4 See any biblical concordance for noting the frequency of these terms.

5 Michael Fishbane, *The Kiss of God: Spiritual and Mystical Death in Judaism*, Seattle: University of Washington Press, 1994, pp. 19–20; quoted in Edmée Kingsmill SLG, *The Song of Songs and the Eros of God*, Oxford: Oxford University Press, 2009, p. 198.

6 Benedicta Ward, 'Spiritual Marriage', in Gordon Wakefield (ed.), *The Westminster Dictionary of Christian Spirituality*, London: SCM Press, 1983, pp. 259–60.

7 Isa. 54.6; Hos. 1.2; 2.2, 19–20.

8 Already referred to in Chapter 1.

9 Andrew Louth, *Origins of the Christian Mystical Tradition*, Oxford: Clarendon Press, 1981, pp. 54–5.

10 Quoted in Bernard McGinn, *Foundations of Mysticism*, Vol. 1, New York: Crossroad, 1991, p. 117.

11 Rom. 8.4, for example.

12 Essay on Origen by Kallistos Ware and Andrew Louth, in Kim Nataraja (ed.), *Journey to the Heart*, London: Canterbury Press, 2011, p. 57.

13 Origen, *The Song of Songs: Commentary and Homilies*, trans. R. P. Lawson, London: Longmans Green, 1957, p. 29.

14 See Part 2, Song 2.5; 5.8.

15 Ambrose, *On Isaac* 4.11, in C. Shenkl (ed.) *Sancti Ambrosii Opera*, Vienna, 1895; Song 1.4, cf. 2 Cor. 12.2ff.

16 Ambrose, *On Isaac* 6.50.

17 See also Part 2, Song 1.2.

18 For this section, I am indebted to Bernard McGinn's *Foundations of Christian Mysticism*, p. 211.

19 McGinn, *Foundations of Christian Mysticism*, p. 140.

20 See Gregory of Nyssa, *Commentary on the Song of Songs*, trans. Casimir McCambley, Brookline, MA: Hellenic College Press, 1987, p. 59.

21 Quoted by McGinn, *Foundations of Christian Mysticism*, p. 141.

22 *Homilies on the Gospels* 1.9, quoted in Preface to Arthur Holder (trans. and ed.), *The Venerable Bede on the Song of Songs*, New York: Paulist Press, 2011, p. xiii.

23 Preface to *The Venerable Bede on the Song of Songs*, p. xv.

24 Song 5.13. See *The Venerable Bede on the Song of Songs*, p. 162.

25 Benedicta Ward, Preface to *The Venerable Bede on the Song of Songs*, p. xvi, and throughout.

26 Song 3.1; see Bernard of Clairvaux on the Song of Songs, Sermon 75, I.1. The biblical quotations here are all translations from the Bible used by Bernard, that is, the Latin Vulgate.

27 Matt. 7.7.

28 Isa. 55.6.

29 John 7.34.

30 John 9.4.

31 See Part 2, Song 3.1.

32 Bernard of Clairvaux, Sermon 75, IV.9.

33 *The Collected Works of St Teresa of Avila*, Vol. 1, trans. K. Kavanaugh and O. Rodriguez, Washington, DC: ICS Publications, 1980, p. 210.

34 *Collected Works*, p. 215.

35 *Collected Works*, p. 218.

36 See Part 2, Song 1.2.

37 *Collected Works*, pp. 221–2.

38 *Collected Works*, p. 221.

39 *Collected Works*, p. 236.

40 *The Collected Works of St Teresa of Avila*, Vol. 2, *Meditations on the Song of Songs*, trans. Kieran Kavanaugh and Otilio Rodriguez, Washington, DC: ICS Publications, 1980, p. 242.

41 Peter M. Tyler, 'St John of the Cross' in *Journey to the Heart*, p. 303.

42 Tyler, 'St John of the Cross', p. 70.

43 See Graeme Watson, *Strike the Cloud: Understanding and Practising the Teaching of the Cloud of Unknowing*, London: SPCK, 2011, especially Chapter 3.

44 See Song 2.5; 5.8; see also commentary in Part 2.

45 *The Spiritual Canticle*, verses 1, 7, 9, translated by Peter Tyler, 'St John of the Cross', p. 40.

Part 2: Text, commentary and reflections

1

1 See Chapter 3.

2 In 70 CE, Jerusalem and its Temple were destroyed, during the reign of the Roman emperor Titus.

3 See Chapter 3, p. 18.

4 Priest-Monk Silouan, 'A Century on the Song of Songs', in *Wisdom Songs*, New York: Theotokos Press, 2011, p. 105.

5 Song 2.5; 5.7.

6 *New English Hymnal*, 86.

2

1 See Chapter 3, 'Metaphor and allegory'.

2 John 12.3ff. See commentary on Song 1.12.

3

1 Isa. 1.20; 34.16; 40.5; Jer. 9.12; 9.20; 23.16; Ezek. 33.7; Mic. 4.4.

2 For example, 2 Cor. 11.2; Eph. 4.11ff; Col. 1.18.

3 See Chapter 4.

4 *The Poems of Rowan Williams*, Oxford: Perpetua Press, 2002, p. 8. His poems include a translation of Ann Griffiths' 'Hymn for the Mercy Seat',

pp. 82–3, of which this is the last stanza. Compare the Song at 2.1–7. There is also a reference to Psalm 2.11, 'kiss the Son'.

4

1 Hos. 11.4; Jer. 31.3, in the translation by Edmée Kingsmill SLG in *The Song of Songs and the Eros of God*, Oxford: Oxford University Press, 2009.

5

1 See Job 30.30: 'My skin turns black . . . my lyre is turned to mourning'; and Lam. 4.8.
2 Ps. 120.5.
3 2 Chron. 3.14.
4 Song 8.8.
5 Luke 2.51.
6 Luke 1.46–55.

6

1 For example, Jer. 3.13.
2 Lam. 1.8.
3 Luke 13.34.
4 Jer. 3.12.
5 Jer. 3.15.
6 See Rom. 11.28–32.
7 Ps. 51.1–4, 7, 9–12.

7

1 See Chapter 3; and commentary on Song 1.2–4.
2 Wisd. 7.25–29.
3 Wisd. 8.9.
4 Song 6.4.
5 Gal. 4.25–26; Rev. 21.2ff.
6 Rev. 21.3–5.

8

1 1 Cor. 1.20–25.
2 He is now generally known as Pseudo-Dionysius. Originally taken to be Dionysius the Areopagite of Acts 17.34, by the sixteenth century he was recognized to be a sixth-century monk deeply influenced by Neo-Platonism.

9

1 Song 8.13.
2 Pss. 43.3; 46.5; 84.2.
3 Jer. 23.1ff.; Ezek. 34.1–10.
4 John 10.11ff.
5 John 10.11.

10

1 Ps. 19.10.
2 Ps. 12.6.
3 Ps. 19.7–8.
4 Ps. 119.1, 35, 40.
5 Stephen B. Dawes, *SCM Study Guide to the Psalms*, London: SCM Press, 2010, p. 145.

11

1 Mark 14.3.
2 Mark 14.6–9.
3 Matt. 26:6ff; Luke 7.36–50; John 12.3–8.
4 John 12.7–8.
5 Song 1.3.
6 John Cassian (*c*.360–440), *Conferences* IV.5.
7 Benedictines of Stanbrook, *Minor Works of St Teresa of Avila*, 1913, p. 158.

12

1 Dom Bede Griffiths OSB (1906–93).
2 Peter Spink (ed.), *The Universal Christ: Daily Readings with Bede Griffiths*, London: Darton, Longman and Todd, 1990, p. 47.
3 Shirley du Boulay, *Beyond the Darkness: A Biography of Bede Griffiths*, Alresford: O Books: 2003, p. 193.
4 D. H. Lawrence, *Women in Love*, London: Penguin, 1995, p. 365.
5 Spink, *Universal Christ*, p. 23.

13

1 Isa. 35.2.
2 Hos. 14.4, 5, 7.
3 Translated by Ursula Vaughan Williams.

14

1 Marvin H. Pope, *Song of Songs*, New York: Yale University Press, 1977, pp. 371–2.
2 Gal. 5.22–23.

15

1 2 Sam. 6.16.
2 Rev. 19.9.
3 Post Communion Prayer for the Feast of All Saints, *Common Worship*, copyright The Archbishops' Council of the Church of England, 2000.

16

1 For Origen, see Chapter 4.
2 Origen, *The Song of Songs*, trans. R. P. Lawson, London: Longmans Green, 1957, p. 29.
3 Ps. 13.1.
4 Ps. 22.2.
5 Ps. 88.13–14.

17

1 Robert Johnson, *He: Understanding Masculine Psychology*, New York: Harper, 1997, quoted in Peter M. Tyler, *St John of the Cross*, London: Continuum, 2010, p. 41.
2 St John of the Cross, *The Living Flame of Love*, 2.8.

18

1 Ellen F. Davis, *Proverbs, Ecclesiastes, and the Song of Songs*, Louisville, KY: Westminster John Knox Press, 2000, p. 252; also Edmée Kingsmill SLG, *The Song of Songs and the Eros of God*, Oxford: Oxford University Press, 2009, p. 239.
2 Davis, *Proverbs, Ecclesiastes, and the Song of Songs*, p. 252; also Kingsmill, *Song of Songs*, pp. 240–1.

19

1 Qur'an, Sura 100.
2 Edmée Kingsmill SLG, *The Song of Songs and the Eros of God*, Oxford: Oxford University Press, 2009, p. 241.
3 Rosa Giorgi, *Saints in Art*, Los Angeles: J. Paul Getty Museum, 2002, quoted in Kathleen Martin (ed.), *The Book of Symbols*, Cologne: Taschen, 2010.
4 Marie Louise von Franz, *The Interpretation of Fairy Tales*, Dallas: Spring Publications, 1970, quoted in Martin, *The Book of Symbols*.
5 *Tsva'ot* – gazelles; *aylot hassadeh* – wild does.
6 Ellen F. Davis, *Proverbs, Ecclesiastes, and the Song of Songs*, Louisville, KY: Westminster John Knox Press, 2000, pp. 253–4.
7 Song 3.5.

8 Gregory of Nyssa, *Commentary on the Song of Songs*, trans. Casimir McCambley, Brookline, MA: Hellenic College Press, 1987, pp. 194–5.
9 *The Cloud of Unknowing and Other Works*, trans. A. C. Spearing, London: Penguin, 2001, p. 25 (my italics).
10 *Cloud of Unknowing*, p. 28. See also Graeme Watson, *Strike the Cloud*, London: SPCK, 2011, esp. pp. 10–11, 'A naked intent unto God'.

20

1 See also her poem 'Hymn for the Mercy Seat' above (commentary on Song 1.1–4).
2 Song 5.10.
3 *The Poems of Rowan Williams*, Oxford: Perpetua Press, 2002, p. 84.

21

1 Jer. 7.34; 16.9; 25.10; 33.11.
2 Song 2.10, 13.
3 Isa. 60.1. These prophecies come from the time of the exile in Babylon, long after the original Isaiah.
4 Ps. 27.8.
5 Isa. 55.1–4.
6 Priest-Monk Silouan, *Wisdom Songs: A Century on the Song of Songs*, No. 35, New York: Theotokos Press, 2011.

22

1 See commentary on Song 2.1–2.
2 Isa. 35.2.
3 Hos. 14.4, 5, 7.
4 Jer. 32.1–25.
5 'If Aslan represented the immaterial Deity, he would be an allegorical figure. In reality, however, he is an invention giving an imaginary answer to the question, "What might Christ become like if there really were a world like Narnia and He chose to be incarnate and die and rise again in that world as He actually has done in ours?"' *Letters of C. S. Lewis*, ed. E. Warren Lewis, London: Geoffrey Bles, 1966, p. 283, 'A letter to a lady'.
6 Demean = demeanour.
7 Quick'ning = giving life to.
8 Glide = slip away gently.
9 Prove = experience.

23

1 Rev. 3.19–20.
2 Mark 1.10; Matt. 3.16; Luke 3.22.

3 Song 2.12, Jewish Talmud.
4 Gen.1.2, Babylonian Talmud from the time of the exile.
5 Trans. J. Brownlie (1857–1925), *Hymns Ancient and Modern, New Standard*, 158.

24

1 Arthur Holder (trans. and ed.), *The Venerable Bede on the Song of Songs*, New York: Paulist Press, 2011, p. 83.
2 *New English Hymnal*, 360.

25

1 See Song 4.6.
2 *Hymns Ancient and Modern, New Standard*, 394, verses 1 and 3.

26

1 Deut 6.5; Mark 12.28–30.
2 Deut. 4.29.
3 Jer. 29.13.
4 Isa. 65.1.
5 Pss. 4.4; 149.5.
6 *The Collected Works of St Teresa of Avila*, trans. K. Kavanaugh and O. Rodriguez, 2nd edn, *Life*, 37.8, Washington, DC: ICS Publications, 1987.

27

1 See Song 8.8ff.
2 Song 7.10.
3 Hos. 2.5.
4 Matt. 23.37–39; Luke 11.45ff.

28

1 See Ellen F. Davis, *Proverbs, Ecclesiastes, and the Song of Songs*, Louisville, KY: Westminster John Knox Press, 2000, pp. 260ff.
2 Jer. 2.2. Compare commentary on the similar verse, Song 8.5.
3 *New English Hymnal*, 313.

29

1 Rabbinic texts, *Minor Tractates: b. Soferim*.
2 1 Kings 5.5–6; see also 2 Chron. 2.1.
3 1 Chron. 22.14.
4 Ps. 21.1–4.

5 Edmée Kingsmill SLG, *The Song of Songs and the Eros of God*, Oxford: Oxford University Press, 2009, pp. 251–2.

6 Trans. J. M. Neale, *New English Hymnal*, 432, verses 1 and 3.

30

1 On the exuberance of the language of love, see Chapter 2, pp. 9–13.

2 Song 1.5.

3 Gen. 29—31.

4 Gen. 31.21, 23, 25–55.

5 C. Morray-Jones, 'The Body of the Glory' in C. Rowland with C. Morray-Jones (eds), *The Mystery of God: Early Christian Mysticism and the New Testament*, Leiden: Brill, 2009, pp. 504–5, quoted in Edmée Kingsmill SLG, *The Song of Songs and the Eros of God*, Oxford: Oxford University Press, 2009, p. 254.

31

1 The Aramaic translation and commentary on the Hebrew Bible.

2 Sirach 42.24; 33.15; cf. Gen. 2.22–24. On the occasion of my nephew's wedding in Sicily, during which chapter 2 of the Song of Songs was read, the priest also pointed out the aptness of this metaphor in Genesis. The woman is created from the part of the man's body that includes the heart, so that their two hearts would beat together.

3 1 Macc. 4.57; see also Ezek. 27.10–11.

4 Eph. 5.25–27, my italics.

5 *Hymns Ancient and Modern, New Standard*, 170.

32

1 Ellen F. Davis, *Proverbs, Ecclesiastes, and the Song of Songs*, Louisville, KY: Westminster John Knox Press, 2000, p. 266.

2 1 Kings 6—7.

3 See commentary on Song 2.8ff.

4 Davis, *Proverbs, Ecclesiastes, and the Song of Songs*, p. 267.

5 There are textual problems concerning the other names. Amana is a river, not a mountain peak. Senir may be another name for Hermon. See Edmée Kingsmill SLG, *The Song of Songs and the Eros of God*, Oxford: Oxford University Press, 2009, pp. 150–1.

6 From the *Epic of Gilgamesh*.

7 Davis, *Proverbs, Ecclesiastes, and the Song of Songs*, p. 268.

8 Isa. 60.13.

9 Matt. 16.13ff; Mark 8.27ff; Luke 9.18ff.

10 Richard B. Hays, *The Moral Vision of the New Testament*, Edinburgh: T & T Clark, 1996, p. 79.

11 John 14.6.

33

1 See Lev. 18.9.
2 For example, Song 1.9–17; 5.1–9; 7.6–9; 8.1–4.
3 See Chapter 2.
4 Ellen F. Davis, *Proverbs, Ecclesiastes, and the Song of Songs*, Louisville, KY: Westminster John Knox Press, 2000, p. 26.
5 Gen. 32.22ff.
6 From his poem 'Prayer I'.
7 Luke 18.1–8.
8 John Donne, *Holy Sonnets*, xiv.

34

1 The early Greek translation of the Jewish Scriptures.
2 Paula Gooder, *Heaven*, London: SPCK, 2011, pp. 74–5. This book is a most illuminating study of the subject of Paradise.
3 Rev. 2.7.
4 See commentary on Song 4.1ff.
5 Gordon Wenham, *Genesis 1–15*, Waco, TX: Word Books, 1987, pp. 61, 76, 84, 86, quoted in Edmée Kingsmill SLG, *The Song of Songs and the Eros of God*, Oxford: Oxford University Press, 2009, p. 156.
6 See Margaret Barker, *The Gate of Heaven: The History and Symbolism of the Temple in Jerusalem*, London: SPCK, 1991, p. 2.
7 Trans. J. M. Neale, *New English Hymnal*, 204; compare 'Christ is made the sure foundation', also *c.* seventh century and trans. J. M. Neale, *New English Hymnal*, 205.

35

1 Margaret Barker, quoted in Edmée Kingsmill SLG, *The Song of Songs and the Eros of God*, Oxford: Oxford University Press, 2009, p. 158.
2 Ezek. 47.1.
3 Trans. J. M. Neale, *New English Hymnal*, 381, verses 1, 2 and 4.

36

1 Rev. 21.1ff.
2 G. B. Caird, *The Revelation of St John the Divine*, 2nd edn, London: A & C Black, 1984, p. 280.
3 Isa. 12.3; Pss. 87.7; 36.8–10.
4 John 4.10, 14.

5 Ps. 36. Michael Fishbane, *The Well of Living Water: A Biblical Motif and its Ancient Transformations*, Winona Lake, IN: Eisenbrauns, 1992, quoted in Edmée Kingsmill SLG, *The Song of Songs and the Eros of God*, Oxford: Oxford University Press, 2009, p. 163.

6 *Maintzich Gesangbuch* (1661), trans. Ray Palmer (1808–87) and others, *Hymns and Psalms*, London: Methodist Publishing House, 1983, 620.

37

1 Ellen F. Davis, *Proverbs, Ecclesiastes, and the Song of Songs*, Louisville, KY: Westminster John Knox Press, 2000, p. 269.

2 2 Kings 25.13–17.

3 Joel 1.8–12.

4 Exod. 28.33–35.

5 For example, Article XXVI: Of the Unworthiness of the Ministers, which hinders not the effect of the Sacrament, Thirty-Nine Articles of Religion, Church of England Book of Common Prayer (1662).

38

1 Ellen F. Davis, *Proverbs, Ecclesiastes, and the Song of Songs*, Louisville, KY: Westminster John Knox Press, 2000, pp. 276–7.

2 *Summa Theologica*, Part II, question 35.

3 Verses 1, 2, 4, 6 and 7.

39

1 *The Collected Works of St Teresa of Avila*, vol. 2, *Meditations on the Song of Songs*, trans. Kieran Kavanaugh and Otilio Rodriguez, Washington, DC: ICS Publications, 1980, p. 252.

2 Quoted in Edmée Kingsmill SLG, *The Song of Songs and the Eros of God*, Oxford: Oxford University Press, 2009, p. 208.

3 Words attributed to Simone Weil (1909–43), philosopher, theologian and mystic.

4 U. A. Fanthorpe, *New and Collected Poems*, London: Enitharmon Press, 2010, verse 1.

40

1 Jer. 31.20, trans. Ellen F. Davis, in *Proverbs, Ecclesiastes, and the Song of Songs*, Louisville, KY: Westminster John Knox Press, 2000, p. 277.

2 Isa. 63.15, trans. Ellen F. Davis, in *Proverbs, Ecclesiastes, and the Song of Songs*, p. 278.

3 Exod. 30.22–33; cf. Mark 14.3, 8; 15.23; John 19.39. See commentary on Song 1.1–4.

41

1 See commentary on Song 2.5.
2 Ellen F. Davis, *Proverbs, Ecclesiastes, and the Song of Songs*, Louisville, KY: Westminster John Knox Press, 2000, p. 279.
3 Ezek. 22.2; 24.6, 9.
4 See Lam. 1.8–9, for example.
5 Matt. 23.37.
6 Ps. 55.9–11, 13.
7 See Song 2.5 and commentary.

42

1 Ellen F. Davis, *Proverbs, Ecclesiastes, and the Song of Songs*, Louisville, KY: Westminster John Knox Press, 2000, p. 283.
2 Lev. 26.12; cf. Exod. 6.7; Ezek. 36.28; 37.27.
3 Rabbi Akiva; see Chapter 3. Akiva died in the second Jewish revolt in 135 CE.
4 Song 5.9.
5 Song 5.10.
6 Clifton Wolters, *The Cloud of Unknowing and Other Works*, London: Penguin, 1961, p. 230.
7 St Augustine of Hippo, *Confessions*, Book 10, xxvii, trans. F. J. Sheed, London: Sheed and Ward, 1984.

43

1 2 Kings 4.8–37.
2 Jer. 31.21; cf. Ps. 116.1, 7: 'I love the LORD . . . Return, O my soul, to your rest, for the LORD has dealt bountifully with you.'
3 Jer. 31.31–32.

44

1 Gen. 3.16.
2 Gen. 2.18: 'I will make him a helper as his partner.'
3 Rom. 6.6: 'we might no longer be enslaved to sin'.
4 St Augustine of Hippo, *Tractates on the Gospel of John 15.12*, trans. J. W. Rettig, in *The Fathers of the Church*, Washington, DC: Catholic University of America Press, 1988, p. 85.
5 *Hymns Ancient and Modern, New Standard*, 496, verses 4–6.
6 Ellen F. Davis, *Proverbs, Ecclesiastes, and the Song of Songs*, Louisville, KY: Westminster John Knox Press, 2000, p. 295.
7 Mechthild of Magdeburg (*c.*1207–82), *The Love of God in Five Points* (Book 1.17).

45

1 Song 3.1–4; 5.5–8.
2 Quoted by Marvin H. Pope, *Song of Songs*, New York: Yale University Press, 1977, p. 658.
3 Prov. 7.12–18. For more details on this theme see Chapter 3.
4 Exod. 30.25.
5 See commentary in section 37 (4.13–14), 'Pomegranates and spices'.

46

1 Jer. 2.2.

47

1 Jer. 22.24–25.
2 Hag. 2.23.
3 Ellen F. Davis, *Proverbs, Ecclesiastes, and the Song of Songs*, Louisville, KY: Westminster John Knox Press, 2000, p. 297.
4 Rev. 2.17.
5 Compare Rev. 3.12; 14.3. See G. B. Caird, *The Revelation of St John the Divine*, 2nd edn, London: A & C Black, 1984, p. 42; also Heb. 9.4 for the reference to manna preserved, and 2 Macc. 2.4–8 for Jeremiah's declaration.

48

1 Ellen F. Davis, *Proverbs, Ecclesiastes, and the Song of Songs*, Louisville, KY: Westminster John Knox Press, 2000, p. 296.
2 Davis, *Proverbs, Ecclesiastes, and the Song of Songs*, p. 296.
3 Church of England *Common Worship*, Order One: Eucharistic Prayer G.
4 1 Cor. 15.54; cf. Isa. 25.8.
5 Davis, *Proverbs, Ecclesiastes, and the Song of Songs*, p. 297.
6 Deut. 4.24; Heb. 12.28–29.
7 *New English Hymnal*, 137.

49

1 Zech. 2.5.
2 David F. Ford, *Christian Wisdom*, Cambridge: Cambridge University Press, 2007, chapter 10, esp. p. 369.
3 Ford, *Christian Wisdom*, p. 389.

50

1 St Augustine of Hippo, *Confessions*, Book 1.1–2; 2.5.
2 Blaise Pascal (1623–62), French mathematician and philosopher.

Select bibliography

Modern commentaries

Chana Bloch and Ariel Bloch, *The Song of Songs: The World's First Great Love Poem*, New York: Random House, 2006.

Ellen F. Davis, *Proverbs, Ecclesiastes, and the Song of Songs*, Louisville, KY: Westminster John Knox Press, 2000.

Cheryl Exum, *Song of Songs: A Commentary*, Louisville, KY: Westminster John Knox Press, 2005.

Edmée Kingsmill SLG, *The Song of Songs and the Eros of God: A Study in Biblical Intertexuality*, Oxford: Oxford University Press, 2009.

Marvin H. Pope, *Song of Songs: A New Translation with Introduction and Commentary*, New York: Yale University Press, 1977.

Priest-Monk Silouan, *Wisdom Songs*, New York: Theotokos Press, 2011.

Historic commentaries

Venerable Bede, *On the Song of Songs and Selected Writings*, trans. and ed. Arthur Holder, with Preface by Benedicta Ward, New York: Paulist Press, 2011.

Bernard of Clairvaux, *On the Song of Songs*, Kalamazoo, MI: Cistercian Publications, 1980.

Bernard of Clairvaux, *On Loving God and Selections from Sermons on the Song of Songs*, ed. Hugh Martin, London: SCM Press, 1959.

The Collected Works of St Teresa of Avila, Vol. 2, *Meditations on the Song of Songs*, trans. Kieran Kavanaugh and Otilio Rodriguez, Washington, DC: ICS Publications, 1980.

Other books and resources cited or consulted

Margaret Barker, *The Gate of Heaven: The History and Symbolism of the Temple in Jerusalem*, London: SPCK, 1991.

David M. Carr, *The Erotic Word: Sexuality, Spirituality and the Bible*, Oxford: Oxford University Press, 2003.

David F. Ford, *Christian Wisdom: Desiring God and Learning in Love*, Cambridge: Cambridge University Press, 2007.

Paula Gooder, *Heaven*, London: SPCK, 2011.

Andrew Louth, *Origins of the Christian Mystical Tradition*, Oxford: Clarendon Press, 1981.

Bernard McGinn, *Foundations of Mysticism: Origins to the Fifth Century*, Vol. 1, London: SCM Press, 1995.

John Main OSB, *Monastery without Walls: The Spiritual Letters of John Main*, London: Canterbury Press, 2006.

Kim Nataraja (ed.), *Journey to the Heart*, London: Canterbury Press, 2011 (Essay on Origen by Kallistos Ware and Andrew Louth).

Denys Turner, *Eros and Allegory: Medieval Exegesis of the Song of Songs*, Kalamazoo, MI: Cistercian Publications, 1995.

Peter M. Tyler, *St John of the Cross*, London: Continuum, 2010.

Other resources

Contemplative Outreach <www.contemplativeoutreach.org> <www.couk.org.uk>

The World Community for Christian Meditation (WCCM) <www.wccm.org> <www.christianmeditation.org.uk>

For a list of communities and organizations promoting Contemplative Prayer, consult <www.retreats.org.uk/downloads/20%20Silent%20prayer%20groups.pdf>

List of selected poems, hymns, psalms and prose readings